How to Convict a Rapist

How to Convict a Rapist

Joy Satterwhite Eyman, Ph.D.

STEIN AND DAY/*Publishers*/New York

First published in 1980
Copyright © 1980 by Joy Satterwhite Eyman
All rights reserved
Designed by Louis A. Ditizio
Printed in the United States of America
Stein and Day/*Publishers*/Scarborough House
Briarcliff Manor, N.Y. 10510

Library of Congress Cataloging in Publication Data

Eyman, Joy S.
How to convict a rapist.

1. Rape—United States. 2. Evidence, Criminal—United States.
3. Trial practice—United States.
I. Title.
KF9329.E95   345.73′02532   79-3824
ISBN 0-8128-2712-0

To my cherished friend
Jane Cathrine Farmer-Jones
and to all those friends
who helped me so greatly

CONTENTS

*   *   *   *   *

How to Convict a Rapist

1

What is Rape?

How many people are aware that a rapist's past record *can* be introduced in evidence against him at his trial? That a victim, as well as the police, has the right to publish a composite picture or a photograph of the man who raped her, and request information from the public regarding this man? That the persons who acknowledge this advertised information may be used as witnesses against the rapist—especially previous victims, even though they may not have reported their rape? That victims have the right to hire an attorney to prosecute or assist the elected prosecutor? That members of the jury trial may ask questions of any witness while that witness is on the stand? That the acquittal rate of rape and attempted rape—where a jury finds the defendant not guilty—is about 80 percent, second only to that of gambling? That female jurors are more likely to acquit a rapist than male jurors? That the F.B.I. Uniform Crime Report of 1975 listed nearly 8 percent of all homicides are related to rape and *sex offenders?*

RAPE IS A CRIMINAL ACT

The most frustrating problem a rape victim faces after the rape may be "proving" to the authorities, both medical and law enforcement, that she has actually been the victim of a crime. The fight to win a conviction of "Guilty" against a rapist is an arduous and uphill one. But it can be invaluable in more ways than one. It will lock up a dangerous criminal. Moreover, it will give the victim peace of mind. Studies have shown that conviction of her rapist is the single most important factor in reestablishing the mental health and stability of a rape victim.

This book shows her how to gather evidence, illustrates how criminal investigations are conducted, and how a case should be prepared for trial. For many reasons, the methods outlined in this book are impossible for officers to pursue in every case. Most law enforcement agencies don't have the time to prepare an in-depth investigation for each case. But the victim may have both the time and the drive to pursue her case.

AUTHORITIES' HOSTILITY TOWARD RAPE VICTIMS

What often confronts the victim when she reports rape is hostility from the authorities. This hostility is probably projected through ignorance of the nature of rape. Most persons, medical and law enforcement personnel included, still consider rape an encounter in which the victim participates in some way. This feeling persists in spite of the enormous literature about rape that has been written in recent years. To the average person, a rape victim in some way "invites" the encounter. She is not really a "victim."

Hostility toward a rape victim may be unseen and unheard. In fact, most authorities do not suggest aloud that the victim is a participant. They don't have to. Nuances of speech, implications and innuendos, and body language do it for them. There are also still officers and attorneys who will ask the victim if she had an orgasm. This may seem astounding. Rape is a crime of violence and brutality usually accompanied by threat of death. Orgasm would not be remotely possible under such circumstances. But the fact is, the average person may still regard rape as a "sexual" act.

THE DEFINITION OF RAPE

Until recently in many states, the definition of rape was vaginal penetration. But in a vast number of cases the rapist never touches his penis to the woman's vagina. Oral and anal areas are often assaulted instead. Many rapists have trouble obtaining an erection or ejaculating, even in assaults that last for hours. Although they may force all kinds of activity on the female, the penis may never actually touch the vagina.

Rape, in any form, should be classified in law enforcement statistics for what it is—a crime of violence, a crime of assault and battery, a crime of kidnapping, a crime of unlawful imprisonment, a crime of attempted murder. Not a sex crime. Studies have shown that rape is not committed for sexual satisfaction. Nor is rape committed because a victim was wearing suggestive or revealing clothes which excited the rapist. However, it is quite possible that rape may be committed for a sense of power, of grandeur, for the emotional high it gives the rapist. My own research, on over 200 rapists and "sex-offenders" and of the records of another thousand inmates, indicates that rapists are not what the literature about them purports. Rapists have a personality disorder that is distinguished by lack of conscience—the inability to feel guilt.

SENTENCE FOR RAPE

The state statutory sentence for rape is sometimes life imprisonment or death. But the rapist usually receives a lighter sentence. And usually he is paroled before that sentence is up. Few persons realize how often an arrested rapist enters a plea of "guilty" in exchange for a lighter sentence. That sentence may be one year in a county jail. Or it may mean participating in a sex-offender "treatment" program. Evidence indicates that these programs are failures; as one prominent prison psychiatrist has said, "Everyone wants a sex-offender program. But I have yet to see one work." The truth is, rapists are hard-core criminals. And to date no methods have been found to cure the hard-core criminal.

CLASSIFICATIONS AND TYPOLOGY OF RAPE

According to Dr. Ann Wolbert Burgess and Dr. Lynda Lytle Holmstrom, two well-known researchers in the field of rape victimization, not all rapes are "true" rapes. Even in cases where victims have been assaulted and molested, it is sometimes difficult to label the case as rape. After intensive research, these two doctors came up with an entirely new set of criteria based on victim consent: 1) rape—sex without consent, 2) accessory-to-sex—inability of the victim to consent, and 3) sex-stress situation—sex with initial consent. It is the first definition this book will deal with.

BLITZ RAPES

Victims of rapists are set up in two ways: they are either singled out for a sudden surprise attack (the blitz rape) or they are conned into a situation where the rapist then assaults them (the confidence rape).

A blitz rapist appears suddenly "out of nowhere" and is usually unknown to the victim. He preserves his anonymity by masking his face, working under cover of darkness, or attacking from behind. A classic example is the woman walking down a sidewalk, who happens to be in the right place at the right time—as far as the rapist is concerned. He is out looking for a woman, he has planned the crime from beginning to end, and if this woman does not become his victim another one will.

Blitz type rapes can occur anywhere. A woman can be assaulted in a street, in a park, in a doorway, at night or day. When she is driving she may be forced off the road. She may come home and find the rapist waiting. She can awaken to find a stranger in her room, or be attacked by the rapist as she is sleeping.

These kinds of rapes are most often regarded as "true rapes." Even so, it is hard to apprehend and convict a blitz rapist. Julia was a young woman studying for her Ph.D. at a highly respected city university. One afternoon as she was walking home a man in his early thirties stepped out from the doorway of her apartment building, forced her inside, and raped her. Although she reported the rape, the police were unable to solve the case before the rapist had attacked two other women on the same street. And when he was finally imprisoned, his sentence was light enough to get him paroled in three years.

The consequences of the rape were particularly devastating for Julia—in addition to the typical response of fear, despair, guilt, and anger, "My boyfriend couldn't take the fact that I'd been raped. He moved out of the apartment a few weeks later. Those two things combined disrupted my life for years."

CONFIDENCE RAPES

The confidence rapist operates in a very different way than the blitz rapist. Often he already knows his victim—and for that reason is harder to convict. Or he may gain access to his victim under false pretenses—masquerading as an official, an investigator, or simply someone needing information or assistance.

One confidence rapist knocked on several apartment doors before he found one that was answered by a woman. The rapist inquired of the occupant if she knew where another girl, whom he called by name, lived in the apartment building. Trying to be helpful, the now chosen victim told the rapist that she had just moved into this building and did not know many of the occupants. However, she suggested that he try a certain apartment, and unlatched the safety chain to open the door wider in order to point to the indicated apartment. This was the opportunity the rapist was waiting for. He put a pistol to the victim's head, told her not to make a sound—then forced his way into her apartment where he raped and robbed her. (This rapist was on parole from prison, where he had been sent after being convicted of a previous rape and robbery.)

A common type of confidence rape occurs in "singles" apartment complexes, where the residents participate in group activities, or meet around the pool or in the activities lounge. The rapist tests his intended victim by talking with her. If he feels that she is vulnerable, he will make some seemingly innocent suggestion that they go to either her apartment or to his on some acceptable pretext, such as that he is knowledgeable about stereos and it will take only a minute for him to tell her whether her broken stereo has a major or minor defect. Once inside the rapist *proceeds toward his ultimate goal and rapes his victim.*

This type of confidence rapist is one of the hardest to convict. And he knows this. It will normally take several of his victims together to convince the authorities that he is indeed a rapist. But he can be convicted and this can be done on testimony alone, though physical evidence would be helpful. It will, however, take a great deal of courage and hard work by his victims to prosecute this rapist. He operates in the certain knowledge that it is his word against that of his victim's.

Many of the victims of confidence rapists know their attacker—a fact that often complicates matters a great deal—especially if the victim has accepted a date with him. He may work in the same establishment in which she does. Or he may be a neighbor, an acquaintance, a friend, a relative. The assailant uses his relationship with the victim to justify his being in the situation. He then deceives the person by not honoring the bounds of the relationship.

Another type of victimization occurs on college campuses. Living at home, Daphne was protected by her family. But away at college she was on her own. Typical of the first few weeks in a strange environment, part of the adjustment involves making new friends and thus dating students who were merely acquaintances at this time. She had several pleasant dates with a new acquaintance, so when he invited her to a fraternity dance she cheerfully accepted. He told her that the dance would last until after her dormitory closed; therefore, she should check out for the night and stay with the girlfriend of one of his fraternity brothers.

Until the dance ended there was no indication that the evening would not go as scheduled.

However, at the close of the dance, long after the dormitories had been locked for the night, her date informed her that his fraternity brother was planning to spend the night at his girlfriend's apartment. He insisted he get her a motel room for the night. This put Daphne in a quandary. If she returned to the dormitory at this late hour she would have to disturb someone to be admitted. She might be subject to disciplinary action for this disturbance. Even today there are still colleges, especially in the South, that adhere to strict rules. Since she didn't have enough money with her to rent the room by herself, she accepted his offer. The stage was set.

He walked her to the door, but instead of saying goodnight, followed Daphne into the room and asked to rest a moment before returning to the frat house. At this point she had allowed herself to become entrapped. When she repelled his advances, he pretended to leave the room, but at the door he turned and forced her onto the bed. He then proceeded to force intercourse upon her. When she fought him he slapped her face and put one hand on her neck. From then on she submitted.

There is no doubt that this is a case of rape. But it could never be prosecuted as such. At best the police and law enforcement officer would call it "seduction." A similar type of "seduction" occurs with victims of child molesters—80 percent of whom are familiar with their assailants. Often they may be a parent, a relative, or a neighbor. Parents sometimes bring molested children to hospital emergency rooms and report that their child has been raped.

Probably the least understood or acceptable cases of rape are those perpetrated upon prostitutes. Initially, though not always, consenting sex was the situation, and what often "goes wrong" is that the male becomes violent or perverted and frightens the woman. Prostitutes then turn to the police for protection. Or they go to the hospital emergency room where the complaint is listed as rape.

Societal attitudes and the laws being what they are, the prostitute cannot simply walk into the hospital and say that she works the streets and has been badly frightened. However, these women are victims of the sexual confidence game as more broadly defined, and they are deserving of help in their own right. The presence of a prostitute in the emergency room of a hospital or at the police station influences the way many people perceive rape victims in general. She is often dismissed with scorn as "just a prostitute who didn't get paid."

In truth, rape is a fact of life for prostitutes, a hazard of the profession. Few prostitutes ever report the rape unless they have been viciously beaten or badly frightened, or have been forced to report the rape by others. Although the rapist may be identified and charged, prostitutes are very rarely willing to prosecute. Rapists know this, and for that reason many rapists prey only upon prostitutes.

Even with a well-defined typology of rape, confusion still persists. It will take a great deal of time and effort to clear the charge of rape from its history of suspicion. Until then, I suggest that every rape victim follow the procedures and methods of this book. She will insure herself of the most effective rape trial possible, and will very probably walk away, leaving her rapist in prison.

2

The Police Investigation

As a rape victim, a woman may be having her first encounter with the criminal justice system, and in many cases this initial contact will seem brutal. There will be a barrage of questions from officers and investigators. The questions will probably be repeated. And many policemen have not been afforded the sensitivity training proper to this kind of situation.

However, the police need all the help a victim can give them in order to apprehend the rapist. There are specific police procedures that should be undertaken as soon as possible following the report of rape. Although the victim may be suffering severe trauma, mentally and physically, this is the best time to gather crucial data—data that may lead to the conviction of her rapist.

THE DISPATCHER'S JOB

If she calls the police immediately, the dispatcher may ask the rape victim questions that enable policemen to begin searching for the assailant at once. Any information she can give regarding the rapist can be relayed to all patrol cars within minutes.

POLICE AT THE SCENE OF THE RAPE

The officers who arrive at the scene of the rape will need enough information to determine whether to arrest the rapist without a warrant—if he is located quickly. The resulting process of question-and-answer can be grueling to the victim. A rape hotline counselor can come in handy at this time—even crisis counseling by phone may ease the immediate effects of the trauma.

GATHERING EVIDENCE

Under the trauma of rape, a woman may not realize how crucial physical data is. Evidence of a sexual nature, such as sperm, seminal fluid, or acid phosphatase, can later help convict a rapist. Therefore, a policeman versed in the procedures of a rape may tell the victim not to clean up, change her clothes, or in any other way alter herself or the scene of the crime. This will allow the police to collect significant physical evidence. Medical care should be obtained (see chapter 3). The police may begin asking questions at this time, and may even take photographs which show the condition of the victim, her injuries, and the scene of the rape. These can later be invaluable before a jury. Even scrapings from under a victim's fingernails may match fresh scratches on the face of the rapist. Finally, the officers themselves will serve as valuable witnesses later at the trial—they, too, can testify to the victim's condition following the rape.

THE POLICE INTERVIEW

After initial questioning, the police will need a detailed report concerning all facets of the rape. This is of utmost importance. It may be months before the rapist is brought to trial, and the facts need to be put down while they are still vivid in the victim's mind. Moreover, the written account can be used to develop the case for the prosecutor.

The report may be prepared in several ways. Police can conduct interviews in the station, or in the woman's home. At her request a friend or relative may be present. Or, if she finds the interview situation too difficult, she can write down some or all of the events. In any case, the most important point is to establish the Modus Operandi (the method of operation) of the rapist. Rapists repeat their crimes, and in the *same manner each time*. For that reason the M.O. is crucial. And everything that happened during the rape forms a significant part of the M.O.

THE WRITTEN REPORT

There are certain procedures that can facilitate the writing of the account.

One of the most effective is a walk-through of the rape—both mental and physical. As soon as she is able, the rape victim should try to recall everything said and done by the rapist. Some men have long conversations with their victims during assaults that last for hours. Everything said by the rapist is significant, and should be written down afterwards—no matter how abusive or indelicate. Certain words or actions may be part of the rapist's trademark, his M.O.

WALK-THROUGH OF THE RAPE

An actual walk-through—going over the road taken during, or en route to the assault, and going back to the site of the rape—will help the victim recall particulars. Although the process may not be pleasant, writing out the account of the crime can often act as a catharsis, freeing emotions that have been immobilizing the victim. The more detailed a report is, the more vividly it will convey circumstances that speak for themselves.

The police will draw up a composite of the rapist from the victim's description. If she is not satisfied with the final picture, she can assist them or draw up her own. It never ceases to amaze me what complete and detailed descriptions many victims can give of their rapist, even when they fear for their lives throughout the entire ordeal. I have seen a victim develop a composite picture—taking only ten minutes to do so—that was an exact likeness of her rapist.

The victim will probably not know the make or caliber of the rapist's pistol or knife, if he had one. But she can go to a gun or sporting goods store and ask to look at their stock and catalogs in order to identify the weapon. This holds true for cars as well. Used-car dealers may have a vehicle that looks like the one used by the rapist.

Some states require as one of the elements of rape that a victim be put in fear of her life. If a weapon was present, this would seem incontestable. If no weapon was involved, a description of the assailant's threats, and his ability to carry out these threats, should be presented. Also, her method of resistance, and evidence of physical abuse will suffice.

QUESTIONS THE VICTIM SHOULD ASK AND ANSWER

The report, once completed, will be turned over to higher-up investigators and detectives. Their investigations will continually refer to this written account. The prosecutor may develop his case from it. To make the report as comprehensive as possible, and to vividly depict the rapist's Modus Operandi, questions such as the following should be considered:

1· Did the victim smell any particular odor—about the rapist or in the area?

2· What was the weather like—foggy, full moon? Weather may be an important symbol for the rapist.

3· What time and what day did the rape occur? Some men are only free at certain times, such as the swing shift, or on a Friday or Monday.

4· What season of the year was it? Could it be an ethnic holiday?

5· What does the victim look like? How old is she? Does she have long hair, good legs, a big bust? Some rapists are attracted to certain specific physical features when they choose their victims.

6· What was she wearing? Blue jeans, pants-suit, a dress, a uniform? Some rapists are attracted to certain types of clothing. It is important to establish what the victim was wearing because some rapists and their attorneys will say that she was wearing a revealing negligee when in fact it was a quilted robe.

7· Details of the weapon the rapist used. (They use an easy-to-find weapon if they have not brought one with them.)

8· How did the rapist approach his victim? Front, back, from the alley; did he assault her in bed while she was sleeping?

9· Describe the exact spot where the attack took place, the location in the parking lot and the kind of parking lot.

10· Did the victim notice any strange men hanging around where she works or lives? Any workmen in the area at the time of the rape or earlier?

11· Did she notice any strange cars? Any man sitting on the passenger side of a car, as though he was waiting for someone?

12· Had there been anyone in the neighborhood asking directions to someone's home or some address that she did not know, especially if she knows her neighbors and neighborhood?

13· Did she notice anything "out of place" even though she can't put her finger on what it was? Was there anyone who alarmed her, a sort of sixth sense of danger or of a dangerous situation? (One of the values of a police officer knowing his beat is that anything unusual, anything out of place, immediately grabs his attention.)

14· Did her neighbors notice anything unusual? Perhaps they will talk with her if they are reluctant to talk with police officers.

15· Did she receive any obscene phone calls or any calls where the caller hung up when she answered? This could be a ploy to make sure she was home. An obscene phone call may be used by a rapist to psyche himself up to go out and rape.

16· Did she make any purchases lately of shoes? Lingerie from a salesman?

17· Did her service station attendant notice any strangers in the area, or hanging around the neighborhood lately? Service stations are a very good source of information about strangers in town.

18· Does she know of any religious fanatics passing through the neighborhood? Religious fanatics are often sex offenders.

19· Did her rapist have any distinctive voice qualities or accents?

20· Was her rapist using drugs, or alcohol? Was he a member of a gang?

21· Did she get any clues as to the occupation of her rapist?

22· Did she notice any lingerie or wire in the rapist's car? Anything unusual in the car? Wire can be used to garrote victims. Lingerie may be a fetish.

23· Did she leave, or "plant" anything in the rapist's car? Or is there something distinctive about the car that she noticed?

24· Did the rapist take anything belonging to her? If so, what? Does she know what he did with it? If he took her underwear, did he use it to masturbate with, or did he slash it?

25· What was the rapist's escape route? Rapists know their areas very well. Find his escape route and it may lead you to the rapist.

26· Did her Rape Crisis Line receive any phone calls that use the same words that her rapist did?

27· Does she suspect anyone? Why, or does she know why? Perhaps she just has a feeling that a certain person could be her rapist. She should tell the police that she has no evidence, only a hunch. The police can rule this person in or out of the picture.

In helping to describe the rapist, many law enforcement agencies have information forms for missing persons, or sex crime analysis units which have descriptions of persons listed, so that the officer only has to circle the appropriate characteristics. If the victim looks at a form such as this, it may help her to remember special areas that she might otherwise overlook. In case her department does not have such forms, the following may be of help to her:

Total number of perpetrators of this crime: _____ .

This is perpetrator No. _____ .

Age of perpetrator: _____ .

Exact age, if known: _____ .

Under 14	35 – 39
15 – 19	40 – 45
20 – 24	45 and over
25 – 29	Unknown – Reason
30 – 34	(Blindfolded; mask; not seen, etc.)

Race of perpetrator:
White
Black
Hispanic/light
Hispanic/dark
Oriental
Brown
Other _____ .
Unknown

Height of perpetrator
Under 5'
5' – 5'4"
5 ' 5" – 5'8"
5'9" – 6'0"
6'1" – 6"4"
Over 6'4"
Unknown

Weight of perpetrator:
Under 100
100 – 124
125 – 149
150 – 174
175 – 199
200 – 224
Over 225
Unknown

Marks/Scars:
Birthmark
Freckles
Moles
Multiple
Pimples/blemishes
Pockmarks
Scars
Other _____ .

Location of Marks/Scars:
(Circled above)
Arm
Face
Hand
Leg
Multiple
Trunk
Other _____ .

Hair Style:
Afro – long
Afro – short
Curly – long
Curly – short
Bald
Partially bald
Kinky
Special cut (styled)
Straight – long
Straight – short
Unusual – Unknown

Hair Color:
Black
Blond
Brown
Grey
Red
Streaked
Other
White
Unknown

Facial Hair:
Beard
Beard & mustache
Heavy brows
Long sideburns
Multiple
Mustache
Other
Unknown

Eye Color:
Black
Blue
Brown
Hazel/Green
Maroon
Mixed
Unknown

Deformity/Unusual:
Arm
Ears
Face
Hand
Leg
Trunk
Other _____ .

Complexion:
Brown
Dark
Light
Medium
Tanned
Other
Unknown

Teeth:
Braces
Discolored
Capped
Gold
Missing lower
Missing upper
Protruding – buck
Visible cavity
Good, straight

Voice/Speech:
Accent – U.S. Regional
Accent – Other
Very low
Stammer/stutter
Lisp
Effeminate, very high
Gruff, harsh
Nothing unusual
Other _____ .

Clothing:
Business
Casual
Dirty, sloppy, torn
Flashy
Gang jacket
Well-dressed
Uniform
Other – specify: _____ .
Unknown

Tattoos:
Arms
Back
Chest/neck
Hands
Legs
Genitals
Buttocks
Other _____ .

Jewelry:
Brooch/pin
Bracelet
Earring
Eyeglasses
I.D. bracelet
Medallion
Necklace/pendant
Nose ring
Ring
Other _____ .

Perpetrator's Actions:
Fetish
Handcuffed
Masturbated
Sexual abuse
Threatened children
Tied victim
Verbal abuse
Other _____ .

Behavior of Perpetrator
During the Act:
Abusive language
Affectionate language
Apologetic
Brutal
Impotent
Other degrading act
Sadistic behavior

Behavior of Perpetrator
Upon Termination of Act:
Apologized
Fled silently
Gave time limit
Suggested future contact
Threat of retaliation
Verbal abuse
Other _____ .

Headgear:
Bandana
Baseball cap
Beanie
Beret
Fatigue cap
Fedora-type hat
Knit hat
Turban/kerchief
Wide-brim hat
Other _____ .

Relationship of Perpetrator to Victim:
Date
Pick up
Hitchhiker
Friend/social acquaintance
Babysitter
Relative (immediate family – incest)
    (father, brother)
Relative (uncle, cousin, etc.)
Boyfriend/girlfriend
Business relationship
Same school
Neighbor
Has been seen in the neighborhood
Nickname known
Full name known
Name and address known
Co-worker
Landlord
Total stranger
Unknown – no information

Unusual/Additional Information:
Drug user
Alcohol user
Gang member
Multiple (More than one of the above)
Other – specify: _____ .

Occupation of Perpetrator:
Clerical, office
Entertainer
Factory worker
Food service worker (cook, waiter, etc.)
Foreman
Health services
Laborer (unskilled)
Laborer (skilled)
Manager, administrator
Mechanic, repairman
Police, fire
Professional & technical

Salesperson
Service worker (custodian, etc.)
Steward
Student
Teacher
Truck driver
Writer/artist
Unemployed
Other _____ .

Modus Operandi:
Con Story:
Requested information
Requested assistance
Offered assistance
Offered job

Presented Self As:
Delivery man
Interviewer
Policeman
Other city official
Repairman
Other con story: _____ .
Break and entry
Forced way into house/apt.
Followed victim into building
Grabbed complainant
Child/adult
Child/child
Taken to perpetrator's residence
Pick-up in building
Accosted with weapon
Performing legitimate service
Other _____ .
Unknown

Means Employed by Perpetrator:
Hand gun
Avowed hand gun
Knife
Avowed knife

Oral threat
Physical force
Chemical or drugs
Toy gun
Machine gun/shotgun
Blunt instrument
Cutting instrument
Multiple weapons
Others _____ .

Vehicle Type:
Auto
Bus
Large truck
Small truck/camper
Motorcycle
Taxi
Bicycle
Other _____ .
Unknown

Vehicle Make:
GM
Ford
Chrysler
American Motors
Foreign
Other
Unknown

Vehicle Body Color:
White/cream/light
Grey/silver
Gold/yellow
Red/maroon
Brown/beige
Black/dark
Green
Blue
Unknown

Body Style:	Station wagon
Sedan	Compact
Hardtop	Sports car
Convertible	Other
	Unknown _____ .

A final note: The rape victim should not let the insensitivity of a few law enforcement officers turn her off her own case. But she must remember that while her case is all-consuming to her, to the law enforcement department she is one of a long line of heartbreaking victims that they see every day. Also, as kind and compassionate as many officers are, they cannot be heroes twenty-four hours a day, seven days a week. Therefore, she must look to others for her emotional support—to her Rape Crisis Center, her Mental Health Center, her family and friends. If there is no Rape Crisis Center or Crisis Center listed in the telephone directory, she can dial either Information or Operator and the telephone operator will assist her. If she tells the operator that this is an emergency, that she has just been raped and needs assistance, the operator will usually stay on the line until help is obtained. If this operator can be identified, he or she can later testify in her behalf that the victim said she had been raped, and any other pertinent information she may have given.

3

Rape and the Medical Evidence

MEDICAL EVIDENCE THAT CAN CONVICT

The right medical evidence, presented in a dramatic and coherent manner, can be enough to convict a rapist. This does not mean simply the presence of sperm or seminal fluid. The precise documentation of scratches and bruises, and other signs of a struggle, can be as persuasive in the minds of jurors as laboratory tests. It is important that this evidence be gathered immediately. Unfortunately, any medical treatment the victim of a rape receives—as well as the collection of medical evidence to be used by the state for a possible court trial—is usually done at the expense of the victim, whereas any criminal in custody is furnished medical treatment at state expense.

The fact that evidential material is being taken *does not* mean that the victim must prosecute. Evidential material is so fragile that it must be taken immediately or it may be lost forever. The decision to prosecute or not to prosecute can be made by the victim at a later date. After a rape all wounds, no matter how slight, should be immediately attended to. The risk of infection is high for rape victims. They are susceptible not only to tetanus and infection, but also to venereal and other diseases.

The clothing the victim was wearing at the time of the rape will need to be examined by the crime laboratory for evidential material to be used in court, in case the rape goes to trial. If possible, the police would like to take the clothing when it is removed at the hospital for the physical examination. For this reason extra clothing should be taken with, or brought to, the victim at the hospital.

Many rape victims will need only short-term medical attention, but most will need long-term emotional support. After a victim has been healed physically she may still need professional help to recover emotional balance.

TESTING FOR SPERM

What will the crime lab be looking for in the way of evidence? Sperm, the male reproductive cells. Also prostatic acid phosphatase, an element confined to seminal fluid and not present in the spermatozoa. When an elevated acid phosphatase is found it means that seminal fluid is present, irrespective of spermatozoa.

DOCUMENTING WOUNDS AND SCRATCHES

Besides the presence of sperm and acid phosphatase on the body and clothing of a rape victim, other physical evidence that may be found include hairs from the rapist's head and body, some of the rapist's skin from under the victim's fingernails if she has fought and scratched the rapist, broken fingernails, grasses and seeds from the scene of the crime if the rape occurred outside—the list is endless.

For comparative purposes, samples of the victim's hair will be taken, as well as blood samples. Blood samples will also be taken to test for venereal disease, etc.

MEDICAL CARE

During the examination the victim may be given medication to prevent pregnancy or venereal diseases. Many physicians fail to tell rape victims that this medication may make them nauseated. Medication can be given to avoid nausea. Victims must be seen again six weeks after the rape, in order to be certain they have not contracted a disease and are not pregnant.

The evidence must be protected from contamination until after the tests are completed. This handling is called "the chain of evidence," which means that there can be no possible way to let any foreign matter get into the specimen before the evidence is tested, or that the specimen cannot be switched for some other specimen. One way to do this is have a small portable lockbox in which the evidence can be stored until it is turned over to the law enforcement agency handling the case.

Surprisingly often, no physical evidence such as sperm is found. The absence of such physical findings frequently detracts from the credibility of the victim's story at the trial. It should be explained that there is a very high rate of sexual dysfunction among rapists. And the documentation of scratches, wounds, bruises, and other physical trauma, as well as the emotional trauma the victim has suffered, can be equally important pieces of medical evidence. They must simply be presented in the proper manner.

The F.B.I. has developed a method of obtaining fingerprints from skin, if the skin is treated within an hour and a half of the incident. It may be possible to obtain the rapist's fingerprints from the victim's body, although to date few agencies have this capability.

Certain physical signs can sell the jurors as easily as laboratory tests. In fact, the absence of these physical findings frequently detracts from the credibility of the victim's story at the trial. One victim I know was asked by the doctor in the emergency room if she had any scratches on her body—instead of examining the victim himself. The victim, still in shock, said "No." When she returned home she bathed and found innumerable scratches on her body. Because this physical trauma had not been medically recorded, it could not be introduced at the trial with any degree of credibility.

If the physician has not conducted a thorough search of the body, the victim's family or friends who saw the condition of her body can testify in court.

If a victim does not even have scratches and bruises to show physical resistance, a timely, believable, consistent medical history is necessary and must be correlated to the victim's testimony. The physician's findings alone may not carry great weight, but in conjunction with a victim's testimony, medical-legal corroboration often determines the guilt of the rapist.

There is no law that states that a physician (medical doctor) must collect the evidence needed for the crime lab from the rape victim. Nor is there a law that states that a medical doctor must testify in a rape case. However, if a physician refuses to testify at a rape trial, through either a deposition or as a witness in the criminal trial, the rape victim may sue the physician in a civil court for breach of contract. When a physician establishes a physician – patient relationship, either by undertaking the care of that person or by serving as a consultant, he or she has the duty to assist that patient in any legal matter pertaining to the patient's medical care—even if unaware of the legal aspects at the time medical care was undertaken.

Actually, nurses are quite capable of taking the history of the rape, the evidence needed for the crime lab, conducting the physical examination of the victim's body and taking photographs of trauma areas, and may testify to this in court.

No accident victim is allowed to bleed to death in the emergency room of a hospital while nurses stand by waiting for a medical doctor to arrive. Neither should the victims of rape be subjected to the agonies of a long wait in an impersonal hospital emergency room for a physician to come to take evidence that can as efficiently be taken by a nurse. And, as a rule, through their attitude and body language, nurses more easily display to the victim that they understand and accept the trauma she has suffered and is still suffering.

Some jurisdictions already use nurses for this purpose. Other jurisdictions use nurses to testify at the trial. When nurses take the witness stand in a rape case, they should be wearing their nurse's uniform. It represents their professional capacity, and projects a positive and capable image to the jury.

For many rape victims this may be their first pelvic examination. Pelvic examinations can be unpleasant. A first-time pelvic examination can be anguishing for a rape victim, and with each subsequent examination in the years to come she may have a flash-back memory of it. Considering this potential flash-back, hospital personnel have a responsibility that may affect the victim throughout much of her life.

Because the crime of rape has rarely been recognized as a medical emergency, there have been few hospital emergency rooms equipped with special handling for rape victims. One of the outstanding rape treatment centers in the nation is the one at Jackson Memorial Hospital in Miami, under the direction of Dorothy J. Hicks, M.D. With Dr. Hick's permission, the following hospital procedures for the handling of rape victims are included.

JACKSON MEMORIAL HOSPITAL
RAPE TREATMENT CENTER

POLICY AND PROCEDURES

INTRODUCTION

1· All Rape Treatment Center activities at Jackson Memorial Hospital will be handled in accordance with the enclosed policies and procedures established in the Emergency Department Procedure book.

2· It is the intent of Jackson Memorial Hospital to protect the patient/victim and keep the anonymity of the situation while complying with the laws of the State of Florida.

3· It is the policy of Jackson Memorial Hospital to encourage the patient/ victim of a sexual assault to notify the police and cooperate with them in apprehending the suspect, if not by name, by situation to possibly establish a pattern or area.

PHILOSOPHY OF CARE

1· To provide the patient with immediate care including gynecologic, traumatic psychiatric, and nursing.

2· To provide the necessary assistance and encouragement in aiding the patient to speak to the proper law enforcement agency.

3· To provide necessary care and appointments for short and long term psychological treatment for not only the patient but others close to the patient.

4· To instruct and provide necessary follow-up care by reexamination and reevaluation of the patient 4-6 weeks after the attack, to be sure there is no pregnancy and venereal disease.

5· To provide the patient/victim with the necessary care and information by a staff specially trained for this purpose.

MEDICAL PROTOCOL:

The Rape Treatment Center physician on call will be notified that a victim of sexual assault is in the hospital. The physician will respond immediately or will refuse the assignment.

A. The initial contacts for the patient/victim will be the Emergency Room nurse and/or a social worker. The social worker/counselor may have obtained a history, but the physician may obtain it directly from the patient.

1· An accurate history is essential. This should not be too detailed. Any variation between the medical and police histories may jeopardize prosecution. The time, place and circumstances of the suspected assault should be recorded. Whether or not a bath and/or douche has been taken since the assault should be documented. Ask if clothing has been changed since the attack.

2· It may be helpful to obtain a past history of the patient's:
   a. menstrual pattern
   b. use of contraceptives
   c. coital experience
   d. psychological behavior

3· The general appearance of the patient should be described and the emotional state and behavior recorded.

4.· The name of the detective and the police department involved should be documented.

5· A female R.N. or L.P.N. must be present during the examination.

6· The time of the examination should be written.

7· Examination of the patient should be extensive enough to include all necessary areas. When possible, a complete pelvic examination should be done.

8· Signs of external trauma should be documented:
   a. A drawing may be helpful.
   b. The oral and anal as well as the genital areas should be included when indicated.
   c. Use Woods light (ultraviolet is useful because semen will fluoresce and may identify areas needing specific attention) on skin, clothing. (Adaptation to the dark is necessary for successful use of this light.)

B. The following procedures must be done:
   *1· All specimens should be labeled properly (see nursing protocols) and initialed by the physician so that they are clearly identifiable as being from this patient. Ideally they should be handed to the police by the physician so that the "Chain of Evidence" is not broken.

   *2· Semen specimens should be collected from the vagina and examined for:
      a. presence and activity of sperm
      b. acid phosphatase

   3· Culture any involved body orifices for gonorrhea; endocervix, pharynx, rectum. The specimen should be plated immediately on chocolate agar in CO_2. Agar plates must be room temperature. (G.C. will not grow on cold agar).

   4· Pregnancy test if indicated.

   5· VDRL

   *6· Venous blood from patient for type and Rh.

   7· Pap test if indicated.

   *8· Comb pubic hair for foreign body, i.e.: Assailant's hair, lice, and place combings in a clean envelope. Label.

   *9· Take scrapings from under the fingernails and place in a clean envelope. Label.

*10· Original clothes are evidence and should be saved for the police. They should be placed in a paper bag (not plastic—spoils evidence due to bacterial overgrowth).

C. After the above have been accomplished, the following should be done:

1· The patient should be calmed and reassured. If necessary, sedatives or tranquilizers may be prescribed.

2· The patient/victim should then be apprised of the possibility of having contracted a venereal disease and the possibility of becoming pregnant. Options as to treatment should be explained clearly.
   a. V.D. Prophylaxis:
      (1) If the patient is not allergic to penicillin: For both Syphilis and Gonorrhea: 1 Gm probenecid orally followed in 30 minutes by 4.8 million units Aqueous Procaine Penicillin, Intramuscularly.
      (2) If the patient is allergic to penicillin: Spectinomycin 2 Gm I.M. (this treats gonorrhea but not syphilis).
   b. Pregnancy Prophylaxis:
      (1) Stilbesterol: 25 mgm bid x 5 days, p.o. The patient may wish a prescription for Benedictin or Tigan to combat nausea.
      (2) Menstrual extraction: The patient should be assured that this is available to her if she misses a period or fails to have withdrawal bleeding after the stilbesterol.
   c. Tetanus toxoid may be given if indicated.
   d. Trauma should be treated as indicated.
3· A cleansing douche may be offered.

4· The patient should be impressed with the fact that a *follow-up visit to her physician or the center is absolutely necessary.* At the follow-up visit the VDRL and cervical culture should be repeated and the patient examined to make sure she has not conceived.

SUMMATION:

1· "Rape" and "Sexual Assault" are legal and not medical diagnoses. Use the terms "Suspected Sexual Assault," not alleged sexual assault.

2· Specifically indicate the trauma: "Contusion," "laceration," "avulsion," etc.

*All evidential material will be given to proper police department if applicable. In cases where patient does not wish to have police intervention, hold specimens for 24 hours—patient may change that decision.

3· Document the presence or absence of sperm; its motility.

4· Remember that the chart may become a piece of legal evidence. Be sure all statements are objective and accurate. Keep a copy for yourself so you can recall the case when required.

5· Leave a Rx for all medications used so that replacements can be procured.

NURSING PROTOCOL

The nurses from the Emergency Room staff are essential to the Rape Treatment Center for several reasons:

1· To provide the patient/victim with support and understanding and explain the purpose of the center.

2· To assist the physician during the examination and to witness evidence collection.

GENERAL RESPONSIBILITIES:

1· When a call comes in via the "hotline," the patient/victim should be encouraged to come to the Emergency Room of the hospital. There the patient will be met by a nurse and immediately escorted to the "quiet" room of the Rape Treatment Center to await the physician. During this time, the nurse will initiate the chart (see *Documentation of Information*).

2· The physician will be notified while the patient is en route to the hospital or as soon as the patient arrives, if no call precedes arrival.

3· Appropriate consents must be explained and signed by the patient prior to examination or administration of medication.

4· The nurse will remain with the patient as long as the patient is in the area unless the victim is accompanied by police. If the nurse is unable to remain in the Center, the patient/victim will be escorted to the family room in the Emergency Room.

5· The patient will be taken to the treatment room for the physical examination. Laboratory specimens will be obtained after the examination. All specimens are to be labeled with keyplated labels, dated and initialed by the physician. Glass slides should include all the information on the keyplate, except written in pencil on buffed edge.

6· Once the examination is completed the patient will be given appointments for follow-up.

7· The patient will be informed of available medications for prevention of venereal disease and/or pregnancy, and possible reactions to these medications.

8· The importance of the four to six week check-up must be reinforced with the patient. The check-up may be done at either the Rape Treatment Center or with a private physician to insure that the patient is free from venereal diseases and has not conceived as a result of the rape. The patient should be encouraged to return to the Center for counseling and support with the Social Worker.

DOCUMENTATION OF INFORMATION:
The nurse is responsible for obtaining the basic information from the patient for the Emergency Room record (Form C210). This record is strictly confidential and kept in the Rape Treatment Center. Accurate documentation is stressed. These records may be used as legal documents.

1· Name and address of the patient/victim

2· Age and date of birth of patient/victim

3· Race

4· Marital Status

5· Local contact or additional ways of contacting victim (i.e., work number)

6· Who present with patient/victim in Rape Treatment Center (i.e., police, parents,

7· Date of incident, time and location

8· Date and time of presentation to Rape Treatment Center (Triage time)

9· Vital signs must be taken and documented

10· Known allergies

11· Description of the observed emotional state of the victim upon presentation

12· The JMH general consent for treatment on back of chart must be signed and witnessed

13· All medication administered to the victim will be documented with the appropriate signature. If the medication is not given, the reason should be indicated.

14· Document all specimens collected

GENERAL HOSPITAL RESPONSIBILITIES:
The Emergency Department will provide the following examination equipment.

1· Linen
   a. gowns
   b. drape sheets

2· Examining instruments—(all disposable if possible) available in a pre-packaged tray.
   a. Pederson and medium size speculums
   b. 12 cc syringe
   c. 3 cc syringe with 2 cc's Bacteriostatic Sodium Chloride (not in pre-packaged tray)
   d. Comb
   e. Non-sterile swabs
   f. Towel
   g. Laboratory slides
   h. Pap sticks
   i. Vaginal aspirate collection tube
   j. Orange stick
   k. Gloves—sterile
   l. Lubricating jelly

3· Medications to be dispensed by physician for prevention of venereal disease, nausea, interruption of pregnancy, etc. (accompanied by necessary prescription)

4· Laboratory vouchers for all requested lab studies

The Dade County Crime Lab will provide the following equipment:
1· Swubes (swabes in a tube)

2· Saliva Boxes

3· Specimen paper bags

The Rape Treatment Center is responsible for notifying the Dade County Crime Lab when supplies are needed.

Dade County Department of Public Health will provide:
1· G.C. agar plates

2· Requisitions for G.C.

3· Zip-lock plastic bags

4· VDRL requisitions

5· CO_2 tabs

RAPE CRISIS COUNSELING PROTOCOL

I. Telephone Contact:

A. The Rape Treatment Center hotline will be answered in the Rape Treatment Center during the day. Appropriate hotline calls will be referred to the Social Worker. The Emergency Room nurses will be responsible for the hotline calls during the evening and night shifts. Only those persons who have been instructed in the proper handling of rape victims will handle hotline calls. Other personnel may answer in the absence of a trained individual and take or give information that will allow contact between the victim and the appropriate staff member (i.e., take victim's name and number, give time when trained staff member will be in further contact).

B. The person handling the call will determine the nature of the call.

1· Log the call

2· Provide initial supportive contact for the rape victim

3· Ask basic date information:
   a. Name of the person calling, if they will give their name
   b. Date and time of assault
   c. Ask the victim about physical trauma
   d. Recommendation and/or referrals

4· Encourage the victim to come to the Emergency Room for treatment and provide information to the victim regarding the services available.

5· Ask the victim for present location.

6· Arrange transportation for the victim through Victims Advocates and ask if the victim/patient wishes the police notified.

7· All calls from the media between 8 a.m. and 5 p.m., Monday through Friday, will be referred to the Public Information Officer. Other hours, weekends and holidays, these calls will be referred to the Administrator on Call.

II. Patient/Victim Direct Contact:

A. Notification of personnel

1· Monday through Friday (8 a.m. - 4:30 p.m.), the Rape Treatment Center Social Worker will be notified by the E.R. staff of the arrival of a patient-victim.

2· During other shift hours, the Emergency Room charge nurse is notified and designates a nurse to handle the patient/victim upon arrival in the Emergency Room. This nurse will remain with the patient/victim throughout the treatment process in the Rape Treatment Center.

B. Arrival Protocols: When the patient/victim arrives in the Emergency Room, the following protocols will be instituted:

1· If the Social Worker is present, he/she will assume responsibility for overall case management.

2· If the Social Worker is not present, the nurse will provide immediate psychological support and arrange follow-up counseling with the Social Worker.

3· Contact police if victim so desires.

4· Arrange to contact relative and/or friends if victim so desires.

5· If the victim requests or if the nurse/social worker feels it is necessary, the victim may be accompanied during police questioning.

6· Counsel victim's family and/or friends if present and advise them concerning the victim's psychological needs.

7· Provide the victim with legal and medical information to the extent permitted by hospital policies and advise when detailed information can be obtained.

C. Follow-up Treatment:

1· When procedures are completed, the Social Worker/Nurse will assess the case and discuss with the victim the availability of further psychological assistance.

2· Appointments will be given as soon as possible, for the nearest working day that there is an opening in the Social Worker's schedule.

3· The Social Worker/Nurse should insure that the victim has been given all information and has had all questions answered before the victim leaves. The victim should be instructed to call if problems arise between Emergency Room discharge and appointment.

4· If there has been physical trauma that incapacitates the victim, the Social Worker will make telephone contact.

III. Counseling Aftercare:

A. The victim will receive a follow-up telephone call or letter from the Social Worker to further assess the victim's condition within 24 to 48 hours. At that time, the Social Worker will make note of the victim's concerns and provide further guidance if necessary.

B. Counseling services are available to the patient/victim and significant others if desired for as long as necessary. The patient/victim will be counseled at the four week follow-up appointment by the Social Worker.

FILE COPY

RAPE TREATMENT CENTER

JACKSON MEMORIAL HOSPITAL   UNIVERSITY OF MIAMI SCHOOL OF MEDICINE

PATIENT'S
ADDRESS _____   BIRTHDAY_____ RACE____M S W D SEP

PLACE OF EXAM_____ DATE:_____   POLICE DEPT. _____ CASE #_____

PERSONAL HISTORY   TIME: _____   OFFICER _____

PARA ____ ____ ____ ____ GR. _____   **GENERAL EXAM:** (bruises, trauma, lacerations, marks)

LMP: DATE _____NORMAL ABNORMAL   NO HISTORY

LAST COITUS: DATE_____ TIME:_____

CONTRACEPTION: YES NO TYPE: _____

DOUCHE BATH DEFECATE VOID SINCE ASSAULT

VENEREAL DISEASE: YES NO TYPE _____RX_____

HEPATITIS: YES NO WHEN_____RX_____

HISTORY OF ASSAULT

DATE:_____ TIME: _____

LOCATION: _____

NO. OF ASSAILANTS _____RACE: B W L O UNK

ATTACKER: KNOWN _____ UNK_____ RELATIVE_____

THREATS: YES NO TYPE _____

WEAPON: YES NO TYPE _____

ORAL ANAL VAGINAL DIGITAL FOR. BODY

TYPE OF SEX: _____

PENETRATION: _____

EJACULATION: _____

Bruise	X
Contusion	C
Laceration	O
Bite	Y
Abrasion	Z

Indicate Areas of Injury

PELVIC EXAM: (include signs of trauma, bleeding, foreign bodies)

VULVA _____

HYMEN _____

VAGINA _____

CERVIX _____

FUNDUS _____

ADNEXAE _____

RECTAL _____

COMMENTS:_____

NOTE: Page 1 and Page 2 of this form is in triplicate and on NCR paper

The copies are distributed as follows:

1. File copy

2. Physician's copy

3. Police copy

JMH-02-5662-6
6-1-76

PAGE 1   SEXUAL BATTERY FORM

FILE COPY

RAPE TREATMENT CENTER
MIAMI, FLORIDA

JACKSON MEMORIAL HOSPITAL   UNIVERSITY OF MIAMI SCHOOL OF MEDICINE

PHYSICIAN _____ NURSE _____ COUNSELOR_____

HEIGHT _____   WEIGHT _____

TESTS

GC CULTURE: ORAL ANAL CERVICAL OTHER_____

VDRL: YES NO (5cc venous blood - red top)

PAP TEST: YES NO

TREATMENT

V.D. PROPHYLAXIS: YES NO TYPE_____

PREGNANCY PROPHYLAXIS: YES NO TYPE_____

TETANUS: YES NO OTHER MEDS: _____

EVIDENTIAL SPECIMENS, TESTING AND RECEIPT

RESULTS OF PRELIMINARY TESTS: A.P.: NEGATIVE WEAK MODERATE STRONG

SPERM: NONE   1-5   6-10   10+   MOTILE   NON-MOTILE

SPECIMENS OBTAINED	**GIVEN TO POLICE**	**OTHER TREATMENT**
10 cc VENOUS BLOOD (red top) _____	_____	X-RAY _____
FINGER NAIL SCRAPINGS _____	_____	SURGICAL CONSULT _____
PUBIC HAIR COMBINGS _____	_____	PSYCH. CONSULT _____
VAGINAL { SMEAR _____	_____	OTHER: (Explain) _____
{ SWAB _____	_____	
CERVICAL { SMEAR_____	_____	
{ SWAB _____	_____	
VAGINAL ASPIRATE _____	_____	
RECTAL { SMEAR _____	_____	
{ SWAB _____	_____	
ORAL { SMEAR _____	_____	
{ SWAB _____	_____	
SALIVA SPECIMEN _____	_____	GIVEN TO POLICE

CLOTHING (number) _____   { TYPE _____
                                   { CONDITION _____

FOREIGN BODIES (number) _____   { TYPE _____
                                   { LOCATION _____

OTHER SPECIMENS _____   PHOTOGRAPHS: YES NO TAKEN BY _____

TOTAL NUMBER SPECIMENS _____   **TOTAL TO POLICE** _____

RECEIPT OF EVIDENCE: THE ABOVE EVIDENCE HAS BEEN RECEIVED BY ME ON (DATE) _____ AT

(TIME) _____ (OFFICER'S SIGNATURE) _____

PHYSICIAN'S SIGNATURE:_____

WITNESS SIGNATURE _____

JMH-02-5662-6
6-1-78

PAGE 2   SEXUAL BATTERY FORM

JACKSON MEMORIAL HOSPITAL
EMERGENCY DEPARTMENT

ANONYMOUS REPORT TO POLICE

DATE-TIME REPORT				DATE-TIME OCCURRENCE	
LOCATION OCCURRENCE:					
AGE	RACE	OCCUPATION		MARRIED	LIVE ALONE
SOBER	HBD	INTOX	INJURIES		
RESULT SPERM TEST				RESULT AP TEST	
IF BREAK-IN, WHERE, HOW					
PROPERTY TAKEN					
OFFENDER IF KNOWN				ADDRESS ˙˙	
AGE	RACE	HEIGHT	WEIGHT	COMPLEXION	HAIR
EYES	BUILD	SCARS		TATTOOS	OTHER
SOBER	HBD	INTOX	FORCE USED		
DOES VICTIM KNOW OFFENDER?				HOW LONG?	
OCCUPATION				EMPLOYMENT	
AUTO DESCRIPTION					
CLOTHES DESCRIPTION					
LANGUAGE USED (ACCENT)				STATEMENTS	

If more than one offender, use extra form for each offender. Use this space for brief narrative what occurred before, during and after assault. Include any additional descriptions, statements and other circumstances.

PUBIC HAIR SPECIMEN _____

PRESERVED EVIDENCE, CLOTHING, ETC. _____

ASSAULT FORM　RAPE TREATMENT CENTER

JACKSON MEMORIAL HOSPITAL

CONSENT FOR ESTROGEN THERAPY

The probability of pregnancy after a single one-time coitus is between one in twenty-five and one in fifty.

Diethylstilbesterol (DES), commonly referred to as the "morning after pill", can be used as an emergency measure to prevent pregnancy. There is, however, still a chance that pregnancy may occur, especially if the medication is not taken exactly as directed.

Diethylstilbesterol is not to be used as a routine birth control medication.

The side effects of treatment with DES may be:

1.   Nausea, vomiting, headaches (the most common).

2.   Late menstrual period, light menstrual period, or menstrual period consisting of spotting.

3.   If pregnancy should occur, the fetus may be affected, and an abortion is advised.

I have read the above and voluntarily consent to taking diethylstilbesterol. I acknowledge that no guarantees have been made to me as to the result of this treatment and will not hold responsible the Rape Treatment Center, Jackson Memorial Hospital, the University of Miami, or the attending physician if side effects or pregnancy occur.

Witness: _____

_____
Signature of Patient

Witness: _____

_____
Date

JMHP-02-5640-3
8/1/78

4

The Legal Process

In order to prosecute a rapist successfully, the rape victim must be familiar with the role of each "actor" in the courtroom drama. She should be versed in at least the rudimentary terms of the law. She must be aware in advance of the countless delays, postponements and frustrations she will meet with on the way. The rapist and his lawyer will use as many delaying tactics as possible, tactics methodically contrived and orchestrated to bring pressure on the victim to drop charges. Trials will very rarely be scheduled at the convenience of the victim. When she arrives at court, she may wait hours before being told that the trial has been rescheduled for a later date. She can look forward to additional weeks of nervousness, sleeplessness, and mounting monetary expenses because of lost work time, interrupted days, and transportation costs.

More important, when she does reach trial the victim will be as much mistrusted and judged as the rapist. Her statements will be viewed with suspicion. The defense attorney will try to trip her up in her story. At times it may be the victim, not the rapist, who is actually on trial.

DEFINING RAPE

Rape is legally both a *crime* and a *tort*. A crime is a public injury, an offense against the state, and is punished by fine or imprisonment. The rapist, in attacking his victim, violates the law and commits a *crime*. A *tort* is a private injury, and the injured party receives money damages as redress. For that reason the victim may prosecute the rapist, *and* sue him at the same time, but in another court, to recover monetary damages for personal injuries she has suffered.

CRIMINAL COURT: THE ACCUSATORY PLEADINGS

Certain legal documents must be filed with the appropriate court in order to bring any criminal case to trial. These documents are referred to as "accusatory pleadings." In most instances the first document to be filed is a complaint. The complaint sets forth the charge against the arrested person, who is now called the "defendant." It is against this charge that the defendant must prepare his defense.

The complaint against the assailant can be signed either by the victim or by a law enforcement officer. If the assailant has been arrested shortly after the rape, the victim is often asked to sign the complaint. This means she must go to the police station or the courthouse to sign the papers the morning after the rape. If the assailant is arrested on a warrant, after an investigation, the law enforcement officer is usually the one who signs the complaint and secures the arrest warrant.

ARRAIGNMENT

No matter who signs the papers, the assailant must be arraigned in court within a limited number of hours, usually the first working day after the arrest. In court the assailant must be advised of the formal charges being brought against him; he must be asked if he can afford an attorney; if he cannot, then a court-appointed lawyer must be assigned to him; he must be asked to enter his plea of guilty or not guilty; and he must be informed whether he will be granted bail and if so, what amount of bail is required.

The victim, in some states, is expected to be in court the day of the arraignment. She may or may not have to testify in court. Some states do not require her to be present at this arraignment. The law enforcement officer signs the complaint and presents any evidence needed before the judge. This is only the first appearance the rapist will make in the legal process, the only hearing where a time limit is set by statute, and the only hearing that she may *not* have to attend.

PROBABLE CAUSE

The second step in the accusatory pleadings is the hearing for probable cause. This hearing can take one of two forms, and may consist of both forms. Some states use a procedure known as a "preliminary hearing" or a "preliminary examination." The proceeding is much like the main trial, although it is heard before a judge without a jury. The accused and his attorney are present and may cross-examine the prosecution's witnesses, and in most instances the defense may present evidence of its own.

This is the court where most of the delays occur. It is possible in some states for it to take as long as a year or a year and a half for the preliminary trial to actually take place. Court calendars, the actual scheduling of trials, may play a part in this delay.

DELAYING TACTICS

Let me explain some of the tactics used by the defense to delay trials. If the rapist is out on bail, he simply may not show up for the trial. In this case, he must be located and rearrested. Since the "clock stops" on the statute of limitations, it is possible for years to go by before the man is located. If he is located in another state, the long legal process of extradition must be gone through if he refuses to sign papers stating that he will return voluntarily with the transporting officers. If he has been arrested in another state, tried in that state, and sent to prison in that state, the prosecutor will often *nolle prosse*, drop the case, rather than spending the money required to transport the prisoner back to your state and to go through the expensive procedure of a trial. This is especially true in rape cases. Prosecutors are only too anxious to use any excuse *not* to bring a rape case to trial. The more time elapsing between the commission of a crime and the court trial, the less likely is the defendant to be found guilty. Important witnesses die or move away and cannot be located.

If the rapist remains in custody while awaiting trial, one of his delaying tactics may be to dismiss his lawyer at the last minute. The judge must then allow him to retain another lawyer, or appoint another lawyer to defend him. An automatic delay is guaranteed in order for the new defense lawyer to prepare the case for the trial. Or the lawyer himself will withdraw from the case at the last minute, allowing the same thing to happen. This is not unknown when the defense lawyer has been privately retained, and paid in advance. The advance money is called a "retainer fee." The private lawyer is often retained with the understanding that he is to withdraw at the last minute. If the rapist has enough money this mode of delay can go on almost indefinitely.

It is possible for the defense lawyer to be legitimately delayed in another court. This automatically gains the rapist a "postponement" or a "continuance." If a witness for the defense, either real or imagined, does not show up for the trial, or is not available that day, a postponement is often granted. *Postponements are also granted by judges to defense lawyers as favors, with no reasons being given or required.*

Probably the most cruel hoax perpetrated upon a rape victim by the judge and defense lawyer, often in collusion with the prosecutor, is the following procedure: After many postponements for the defense, the next trial date arrives and some important witness for the prosecution, such as the investigating officer or the victim, is not present in the courtroom. They may not be present because they have not been notified of the trial date, or they may be out of town or ill, or the defense attorney knows that certain witnesses for the prosecutor will be unavailable on a certain date and he therefore sets that date for the trial. As a result of these tactics, through no fault of her own or of the law enforcement officer, the case is dismissed—and the rapist walks out of the courtroom a free man. Of course, the prosecutor can ask for postponements if his witnesses are unavailable. But he often does not.

The victim does have the right to hire an attorney of her own choosing to assist with the prosecution of "her case." She must, of course, pay the attorney if she hires one. The prosecutor serves her at no charge, as an elected official whose responsibility it is to prosecute crimes. If she does hire an attorney, he can be sworn in as a special prosecutor. The attorney may assist the elected official, or he may conduct the prosecution himself. If more than one attorney is conducting either the prosecution or the defense, all of the attorneys may participate actively in the trial.

And there are steps she can take to force the case to trial. First, she can find out when the grand jury meets, be present at the meeting, and request to be heard. If the prosecutor tries to keep her from the grand jury, she may petition a member of the jury to request that she be heard. A case may also be taken before the grand jury if the judge at the preliminary hearing did not bind the defendant over for a criminal trial. A victim may even petition the Attorney General of the state. The Attorney General is the highest law enforcement officer in the state.

Clearly, the monetary and emotional costs of delayed trials can be prohibitive to a rape victim. If she has moved out of town or out of state she must return at her own expense. Any members of the family, or friends who accompany her also pay their own way. The long-term emotional chaos may cause her to lose or give up her job.

The reality of a rape trial bears little resemblance to television trials. Foreknowledge of the procedures and pitfalls of a court trial can diminish the trauma for the rape victim. Though the tensions remain, she will be able to meet her adversaries on equal ground. This is the beginning of a successful rape trial.

PRELIMINARY HEARING

The second step in the accusatory pleadings is the hearing for probable cause. The victim is required to be present and to testify. As in the main trial, spectators will be allowed in the courtroom at this trial. If the judge decides after hearing the evidence that the rape actually took place (that you really were raped!), and that the rapist may be guilty, he will hold the rapist for trial. This is referred to as "binding the defendant over" for trial or "held to answer" for trial.

When the judge decides to bind the rapist over, the prosecuting attorney will prepare a legal document, known as an "information," to be filed with the trial court. Both the information and the indictment (the indictment is handed down by a grand jury) are very similar in wording, and are also similar in wording to the complaint. All three set forth the crime of which the rapist is accused, the approximate date that the crime was committed, and the place where it was committed.

At present some states have adopted the preliminary hearing procedure, but in most instances the grand jury system will be utilized instead. The United States Constitution in the Fifth Amendment provides that: "No person shall be held to answer for a capital, or otherwise infamous crime, unless on a presentment or indictment of a grand jury." For that reason some states also require the presentation of all serious crimes to a grand jury, although the preliminary hearing, in lieu of a grand jury hearing, has been sanctioned.

GRAND JURY

The grand jury is made up from the same group of people who make up regular juries. There are usually nineteen members in a grand jury. Appearing before the grand jury is not necessarily difficult. The prosecutor and a court reporter will be the only other persons in the room with the jurors when the victim testifies. She will go into the grand jury room alone, tell her story, and answer any questions the jurors may have. As a rule, this jury will not be hostile. If they decide that the accused has raped her, they will return an indictment, the charge against which the rapist will have to defend himself.

The grand jury could decide that the rapist shouldn't be charged with rape, but with a lesser crime such as "attempted rape," which carries a lighter sentence, and this is the charge that will be carried on the indictment. This might occur in a case when a father has molested his daughter. If the grand jury decides that he didn't rape you, they will return a "no bill." This usually means that the case is dropped and the rapist is set free. However, if more evidence is uncovered, or more witnesses are found to testify, the prosecutor may wish to take the case before the grand jury again.

In recent years several states have questioned the good of grand juries and have proposed revisions. In South Carolina, a special study committee has recommended that the use of grand juries in many cases be eliminated because grand juries have become "rubber stamps" for solicitors, as prosecutors are called there. This committee has proposed that grand juries hear only cases involving the death penalty or life in prison, charges against public officials or misuse of public money.

The South Carolina committee agreed that grand juries should continue to exist, subject to the call of a prosecutor, the attorney general, the court, or any citizen who asks for an investigation of "critical issues." The committee has found if solicitors seek indictments, grand juries will grant them. They are equally responsive when requested by a solicitor not to indict an individual. Presently 98 percent of the cases taken before grand juries in South Carolina result in indictments.

Whether a case will be presented to a grand jury or at a preliminary hearing is mostly a decision made by the prosecutor. However, in order to have a preliminary hearing, the rapist has to be in custody, meaning that he has to already have been arrested, although he may be out on bond. The victim, however, can appear before a grand jury without the rapist being in custody, and an arrest warrant can be issued upon the indictment.

If, in the preliminary hearing, the judge decides that there is not enough evidence to hold a trial, or for some other reason refuses to bind the rapist over for trial, the rapist will usually be set free and no further action taken. But, the prosecutor can present the case to the grand jury to see if they will decide differently. Usually he will not take this action unless pressured into it. This, of course, is where the victim enters in.

FUNCTION OF THE TRIAL JUDGE

The trial judge's responsibility is to see that the defendant receives a fair trial, and that justice is done. The trial judge will grant or deny application for change of venue; he will hear a variety of pre- and post-trial motions; he will interpret the law of the case for the jury; he will decide what evidence is admissible and what is not; he will rule on objections made by the attorneys; he will determine the competence of witnesses; and he is supposed to protect the witness from overzealous cross-examination. Actually, his function is much like that of a referee. He keeps order in the court and sees that the trial progresses properly and smoothly.

In many jurisdictions it is the responsibility of the trial judge to impose the sentence to be served by the defendant. A presentence report, which will give him information not available at the trial about the defendant and his previous social and criminal history, assists the judge in arriving at the sentence to impose. When a case is overturned on appeal (sent back for retrial) it is usually because the judge erred.

Unfortunately, many judges tarnish the image and remove much of the mystic connected with the judiciary. In fact, the judge may actually be sleeping on the bench during a trial! I have witnessed this a number of times. That's why some law enforcement officers refer to the circuit court as the circuit circus. While sitting on the bench during a trial, one judge swiveled his chair around and spat a large glob of chewing tobacco out of the second story window of the courtroom. It landed on top of the head of a woman walking into the courthouse. She stomped upstairs, flung open the court-room door in the middle of the trial, and demanded to know who had spit on her head. The judge, without blinking an eye, pointed to the bailiff and told her to see that fellow. After the trial was over the bailiff asked the judge why he had accused him. The judge replied that it didn't look as bad for a deputy sheriff to spit on a lady as it did for a judge!

THE PROSECUTOR

Just getting the prosecutor to take a rape case to court can be a heartbreaking experience for the law enforcement officer. A prosecutor is a publicly elected official, and he tries to take to court only those cases he thinks he can win. Rape cases are "messy." They're not good for his public image. A rape-murder is treated as a homicide, but a rape is still treated as a "sex crime."

Few citizens realize what a powerful position the prosecuting attorney occupies, or just how little education he receives to prepare him for this important position. Customarily law schools require less than 7 percent of their course work to be in criminal law. The other 93 percent of course work is spent in the study of civil law, which constitutes the bulk of a lawyer's case load. Except for a few attorneys who make national reputations as defense lawyers, representing defendants in criminal cases has never been a lucrative field of legal practice.

The prosecutor's range of authority and the crucial nature of his decisions exceed those of any other person—with the possible exception of the judge. The prosecutor makes the decision to charge the suspect with a crime. He determines the nature of the charge, he has authority to reduce the charge by negotiation or agree to a bargained sentence (plea bargaining). He can dismiss the action once it has been filed (*nolle prosse* the case), usually without the judge's permission. It is the prosecutor, who makes innumerable decisions about the prosecution of offenses and who largely determines the course of law enforcement in his community.

The sheer volume of the prosecutor's decisions, the frequency with which the judge and grand juries follow his recommendations, and the relative lack of control on the prosecutor's discretion make his decisions a matter of prime importance. This is frightening when you consider that uncontrolled discretion very often leads to arbitrariness, injustice, and sometimes bribery.

The office of prosecutor may consist of only one elected official dividing his time between his private practice and his duties as prosecutor; or it may consist of one elected official with over 100 appointed assistant prosecuting attorneys. Prosecutors complain that salaries offered prosecutors are so low that young attorneys stay as assistants only long enough to gain practical experience in the law, and then go off to become defense attorneys or to join private law firms. To be elected prosecuting attorney is often considered a stepping stone to higher political office. It would seem, then, that prosecutors come in three varieties: those directly out of law school who wish to work for a salary while they are gaining experience in the practice of law; those seeking a higher political office; and those who are too incompetent to make a living in private practice.

It is the responsibility of a prosecutor to prepare the victim for trial. He should contact her early, explain the legal steps in detail, read back to her the statements she gave police at the time of her assault, and brief her thoroughly on the testimony she will give at trial. However, most prosecutors do very little, if any, of the above.

The rape victim is not usually prepared for the unnerving informality of the courtroom itself. Spectators will be walking in and out and around the courtroom during her testimony. They will be talking to each other and perhaps to the officials concerned with the trial.

THE DEFENSE ATTORNEY AND THE RAPE VICTIM

Dr. Ann Burgess and Dr. Lynda Holmstrom, pioneers in rape victimology, have this to say about defense attorneys:

The main tactic used by the defense attorney in a rape trial is to "blame the victim." The defense lawyer tries to save his client by making it look as though everything that happened was the victim's fault. He does this by focusing on the following issues: (1) Did the woman consent to sex or did she not consent? (2) Did the woman struggle or did she not struggle? (3)

What is the woman's sexual reputation? (4) What is the woman's general character? (5) What was the woman's emotional state at the time of the incident? (6) Did the woman report the rape to someone? (7) Is the woman claiming rape to avoid punishment by parents or husband? (8) Is the woman spiteful? (9) Is her statement that sex occurred accurate?

The defense lawyer's tactics in questioning can be extremely cruel. It is his job to win the case for his client, and he can do this best by trying to discredit her testimony. He will try to mix her up, he will twist her words into a meaning that is not there, will ask questions that cannot be answered by a simple yes or no, and demand that she do just that. He counts on the jury trying the victim, instead of the rapist.

During all of the trial the victim will have to relive the rape, with the rapist near her in the courtroom. Here again she will be controlled, not by physical threats as with the rapist, but by the defense attorney. He becomes the assailant this time. The courtroom is his turf. It is he, not the victim, who knows how the courtroom works. By attacking her verbally he can make her feel nearly as helpless as the rapist did.

Because her medical records—those taken for evidence—are discoverable, and the defense has a right to see them, he will study them and use them against her. Regardless of the contents of the record, he can use it to his advantage. An example of *negative* testimony might be:

"Did you find any sperm?"

"No."

"Did you find any acid phosphatase around the genitals?"

"No."

"Then how can you call this rape?"

The defense attorney will not mention that, although the assault continued for a period of two hours, the rapist could not ejaculate.

The more familiar a victim is with the courtroom procedure, the more in control of the situation she will be. She should study defense attorneys' tactics, especially if she can observe another trial for rape, or a trial in which her rapist's attorney is defending some other person for a crime. In this way she will arm herself for the challenge of prosecuting her assailant.

LAW ENFORCEMENT OFFICERS

Although the prosecutor may appear indifferent to her needs and the defense attorney's attacks are overwhelming, there is one thing a rape victim can count on with even the law enforcement officers who may have been harsh and unkind. They don't like crime and criminals. And they strongly resent the "do-gooder" treatment of hard-core criminals of any age.

Law enforcement officers are the only professionals in the criminal justice system who regularly see the victims and the damage criminal acts have caused. It is the law enforcement officer who talks to the molested child, who sees the results of a gang beating. The law enforcement officer inspects the dead body of the filling station attendant, identifies the young girl killed or mutilated by a drunken driver and then notifies her parents. He is the one to listen to the heroin addict begging for a "fix," and must also comfort the retired couple who have been robbed. No other person in the criminal justice system comes into such constant direct contact with the victim. Actually, few other professionals in the system ever see the victim, except perhaps as a witness in court many months after the crime.

FUNCTION OF THE JURY

It is imperative to understand the function and power of the jury, because the outcome of the case lies in their hands. The purpose of the jury is to interpret the evidence as it is presented and try to determine what happened. Ultimately the jury must ascertain whether the defendant is guilty of the crime with which he has been charged. The jury members will be listening intently to the witnesses on the stand, and attempting to make fair and objective judgments—but they will be influenced as well by the way the victim presents herself, the words she uses and the manner in which she uses them, and how well she withstands the attacks of the defense attorney. All these things can make a difference in the jury decision. The defense attorney is well aware of this. That is why he "cleans" his client before the trial, dresses him conservatively, and coaches him on every sentence that he is to speak.

A criminal trial may actually be either a jury trial or a court trial, where only a judge determines the guilt or innocence of the accused. Although most states allow a defendant to waive the jury and be tried by a judge alone, very few defendants in a rape case waive this right. A trial by jury means (usually) that twelve persons have to be convinced beyond a reasonable doubt that the accused is guilty. A reasonable doubt is one that someone would have after hearing all the evidence in the case and the arguments of counsel, and after applying the law to the case as instructed by the court. If the rapist can plant this reasonable doubt in the mind of only one juror, he cannot be convicted by that jury. A "hung" jury or a mistrial must be declared.

The juror will be subpoenaed to appear at the court on a certain date and time, at which point he or she will be questioned by the judge and attorneys from both sides, and either selected or dismissed. Ultimately, the jury will be composed of a good cross-section of the society in which the defendant is to be tried. This is called "a jury of one's peers."

Unknown to most persons, *the members of the jury have the right to ask questions of witnesses.* Depending on the policy of the judge, they can ask a question directly, or write it down and send it via the bailiff to the judge. This allows the jury to become actively involved during the process of the trial.

THE TRIAL

The prosecuting attorney begins, making an "opening statement" or brief summary of the case and of what the prosecution intends to prove through its evidence. The defense attorney is permitted to make an opening statement as well, but he usually waits until just before he presents his side of the case.

In a criminal trial, the prosecutor always presents his side first. Most of the evidence will be presented through the testimony of witnesses. As each witness is called to testify, he is sworn in, either by oath or affirmation, before he takes the witness stand. Many people do not believe that an oath or affirmation will keep a witness from lying. However, in order to prosecute for perjury, an oath must be given. I know of the "girlfriend" of one rapist who was convicted of perjury and sent to prison because she testified at the trial that the rapist was with her during the period of the rape. The prosecution was able to prove otherwise.

It is not necessary that witnesses be called to testify in the sequence in which the events of a case took place. The prosecutor will determine before the trial how the story can best be told in a logical order, so that members of the jury can understand what took place.

Questioning of a witness by the side who calls him or her is known as "direct questioning," or "direct examination." All direct questioning of witnesses begins with a request for them to state their name, address, and occupation. This is necessary in order to keep the court record of the case complete. During direct questioning, no "leading questions" may be asked. A leading question is one that suggests an answer, such as, "You did have a gun, didn't you?" This must be asked in a manner that will not imply the answer, such as, "Did you have a gun?" However, on cross-examination leading questions may be asked.

During the questioning of witnesses, attorneys for the opposing side will interrupt the proceedings with objections. They may object upon the grounds that it is a leading question, or that it asks for a conclusion from the witness, or because it is irrelevant or immaterial. These objections may be well-founded. However, objections may also be used for psychological reasons—to break a line of questioning or lessen the impact of the testimony that is being given. When an objection is made, the witness may not answer the question until the judge has ruled on the objection. If the judge says, "Sustained," the witness *may not* answer the question. The same question may then be asked in a different manner, or a different line of questioning may be pursued. If the judge says, "Overruled," the witness *must* answer the question.

Cross-examination follows the direct examination of the witness. Cross-examination is done for "impeachment" purposes—to discredit the testimony of the witness or to lower the credibility of the witness. The side that is cross-examining the witness will use any number of tactics to discredit him or her. Attorneys may try to cross up the witness in his or her story. They may try to show that the witness is prejudiced and may not have testified correctly. Or they may cross-examine the witness merely to prove that, as an attorney, they are earning their fee. An attorney may waive the right to cross-examine. However, when the victim testifies, the defense attorney will try every trick in order to discredit her testimony.

When the prosecutor has completed the presentation of evidence, the prosecution "rests." The jury is sequestered in another room. The defense attorney asks for a directed verdict, which means he would like the case to be dismissed for lack of evidence. It is an almost automatic move, and is usually denied by the judge.

The defense then presents its evidence. The defense attorney may decide not to put on any evidence at all. However, he usually does, even though the evidence may be extremely weak. The defense presents its case just as the prosecutor has, through direct examination, with the prosecuting attorney cross-examining defense witnesses.

After the defense attorney has completed the presentation of all of the evidence on his part, the prosecution has the right to call additional witnesses or to present evidence to overcome certain matters brought out during the defendant's portion of the trial.

THE DEFENDANT (THE RAPIST)

A defendant in a criminal trial does not have to present any evidence in his own behalf. This is particularly likely to happen if the defense attorney believes that the prosecution's case is so weak that there is already a reasonable doubt about the defendant's guilt. On the other hand, he may offer evidence in an effort to overcome that presented by the prosecution. This is done in the hope that it will create a doubt in the mind of the jurors, if that doubt is not already present.

The rapist does not have to take the witness stand in a criminal case. He is protected by the Fifth Amendment. If he chooses to testify, he is no longer protected, and in most states must answer every question put to him.

There is an interesting presumption at work regarding the character of the defendant. The law states that the prosecution *cannot attack* the character or reputation of a defendant. However, *if* the defendant introduces witnesses, called "character witnesses," to show evidence of the defendant's good character, then the prosecution may introduce other witnesses *in rebuttal*. The *unspoken* presumption in the case is that the defendant is not of sterling character, therefore, his bad character does not need further attack.

Just the opposite presumption is true of *witnesses*. It is presumed that witnesses have a good reputation for truthfulness, honesty, and integrity. This presumption saves much trial time, for otherwise, before any witness could testify, extensive evidence might be produced to build up the witness in the eyes of the jury.

CLOSING ARGUMENTS AND INSTRUCTIONS

At the end of every trial the lawyers for each side give what is called a closing argument. Here the attorney's salesmanship really counts, for he is asking the jury to believe his side of the case and return a verdict in his favor. These arguments are frequently very dramatic, and unfortunately, and contrary to good judicial procedure, many important cases have been won or lost entirely upon the arguments to the jury.

After the closing arguments, the judge will read his "instructions," sometimes called the "charge" to the jury. These instructions consist of an interpretation of the law and the rules of evidence as they may apply to the particular case. The purpose of these instructions is to assist and guide the jury in their review of the evidence in order that they may arrive at a verdict.

The judge will give the jury instructions on such matters as the elements of the crime involved and, where applicable, the degrees of the crime; the presumption of innocence until proved guilty will be explained; the meaning of reasonable doubt will be reviewed; and numerous other rules will be interpreted which the jury will need to know in order to properly evaluate the evidence as presented during the trial. He will advise the jury that the verdict must express their individual opinions, that they are the exclusive judges of the facts of the case, that they must weigh the effect and value of the evidence presented, and that they must determine the facts only from the evidence received in court.

He will instruct them not to consider as evidence any statement made by the attorneys during the trial and, if objections to questions asked in the trial were sustained, not to speculate about the possible answers. Failure to give certain instructions, or giving instructions improperly, may be sufficient grounds for reversal on appeal.

JURY DELIBERATIONS

The jury will retire to the jury room after they have received the judge's instructions. To prevent any possibility of outside influence on the jury's verdict, they are "sequestered," or locked up, during their deliberations. While the jury is sequestered, a court official known as a bailiff will guard the door and act as their intermediary with the outside world. Legally, the judge may sequester the jury during the entire trial, but this is rarely done. However, after deliberations have started, the jury stays sequestered. Food is brought in to them. Both food and lodging must be supplied by the state when a jury is sequestered. If the jury is not sequestered at night during the trial, they remain together during the day and are taken in a body, escorted by bailiffs, to have lunch at the state's expense.

The first order of business in the jury room is the selection of a foreman by the jurors. He or she will act as chairman and spokesman for the jury during the deliberations. If the jury cannot agree upon a verdict, a mistrial will be declared and the whole trial will have to be repeated with a new jury. If the jury does reach a verdict, the verdict will be read in open court by the jury foreman, in the presence of the defendant. After announcing the verdict the jury's function will have been completed. They will be thanked by the judge and then dismissed.

If the jury's verdict is "Not Guilty," the rapist will be freed immediately of the charge and of custody, and he may not be tried again for this rape upon his victim, even if new and conclusive evidence against him is discovered the next day! The double jeopardy clause of the Fifth Amendment to the United States Constitution states that a criminal may not be tried for the same crime twice.

However, the situation is often more complex. It's very difficult to get a conviction on rape. Robbery is easier, and a rapist charged on several counts is often convicted of only one: A jury may hand down a verdict of Guilty for the robbery but Innocent for the rape.

If the rapist has been found Not Guilty and is later brought to trial on another rape charge, the former rape victim can testify against him at the new trial. Similarly, if the rapist has been tried before and set free, the previous victim should testify at the current trial. At one rapist's *third* trial the prosecutor finally brought as witnesses against him the two previous victims. As the second victim finished her testimony and stepped down from the witness stand, she turned to the jury and said, "If you set him free this time, I hope he comes and rapes every one of you!"

If the jury has found the rapist guilty and he has received a long sentence, the prosecutor may decide not to prosecute on the robbery charge. He may not wish to put his victim through the trauma of another trial, or he may feel that the judge will give a concurrent sentence, rather than a consecutive sentence (a sentence that starts after the other has been served).

If the verdict of the jury is Guilty, the rapist must then be sentenced. This is usually the prerogative of the trial judge, though in some states the jury that heard the case will also decide the sentence. The judge may sentence the rapist immediately, or he may wait until he receives the "presentence investigation." This report will give the judge information not available at the trial about the rapist's previous social and criminal history, and will assist the judge in arriving at his decision on how to sentence the rapist.

The rapist has the right to appeal the verdict. In fact, rape cases are almost automatically appealed by the defendant when he is found guilty. He or his attorney must file papers with the proper court notifying them of the appeal. An appeal hearing will be held where only the prosecutor and defense attorney are present, but this may take many months. While the rapist is waiting he may sometimes remain free on bond. If the guilty verdict is reversed in the appellate court, the trial must be held all over again. If the guilty verdict is upheld, the rapist may appeal to the state supreme court. In some cases he may even go on to the U.S. Supreme Court with a request for appeal. Each appeal may take literally years to be heard by the courts, and during all of these years it is quite possible that the rapist will remain free on bond—and that he will be committing other rapes.

To insure that an appeal does not overturn the original decree, as much evidence as possible should be introduced at the original trial. As an example, we have an appellate judge's opinion when the court refused to overturn conviction of four rapists:

"We hold that if such an error did occur it was harmless beyond a reasonable doubt, because there was overwhelming evidence of each appellant's guilt."

The judge then outlined the young woman's testimony: She dropped one of her shoes at the spot where she was forced into the defendant's car; it was found in that area. She took the keys from the car at the scene of the rape and threw them away when the four weren't looking. She managed to lift the wallet of one of the four and hid it at the scene; she hid her underpants under the car seat; she also managed to hide a wine bottle used to threaten her.

Other evidence cited by the appellate judge included fingerprints, a bottle-cap matching the wine bottle and hairs from the victim, all found in the car.

The judge also pointed to testimony of the owner of a truck used to tow away the key-less car and the positive identification of two of the assailants by the victim.

CIVIL SUITS

If the verdict of the court is Not Guilty, the victim can still take action against the rapist. She may turn to a civil court and sue her assailant there. She may also sue her landlord or the business establishment where she worked or spent the night (such as a motel) if she was raped on the premises and believes it was the fault of the establishment's inadequate security precautions. Lawyers prefer to take cases concerning an establishment. Familiar precedents have been set, and if a woman is raped in a hotel or motel by a stranger who snuck into her room, the management will probably do everything in their power to appease her. They will often try to settle out of court, rather than risk the bad publicity. A case in point is the civil suit against the Howard Johnson Motor Lodge in Westbury, New York, by singer Connie Francis. In 1976 Miss Francis received nearly $1.5 million in damages from the motel where she was raped. Her civil suit charged that the motel had failed to provide adequate room door locks and other security measures.

Similarly, a female employee of an all-night convenience store was robbed, kidnapped and raped. Not long before, a salesman had tried to sell the owners an alarm for the protection of the employees. The owner did not buy the alarm. When the victim was counselled to sue the store owners she retained a lawyer, and the case was settled out of court. The owners realized at once they were at fault, and wished to avoid the adverse publicity connected with a civil suit.

A woman who has been raped in her apartment can sue her landlord. A precedent has been established in the state of New York against a landlord who refused to put window gates on ground level. A rapist came in this way, and the court decided in favor of the victim.

A civil suit can be brought by a victim against an establishment, even though the rapist may not have been apprehended, or has never even been identified. One female Marine captain had requested that female marines not be required to stand guard duty alone in an isolated, non-secure building. All a rapist had to do was look at the roster and find out the nights female marines would be alone. The captain's request, however, was overruled and the building was not made secure.

One night a female marine on guard duty was raped. She had followed standard procedure and attempted to secure the building before going to sleep on a cot provided inside the building. During the early hours of the morning a rapist slipped into the building, threw a towel over the marine's head, and took control of her before she was able to protect herself. She did notice that he was wearing a jogging suit. On a military base, people wearing jogging suits are rarely stopped and requested to produce identification. Rapists know this is an excellent disguise. This marine victim has grounds for a third-party civil suit.

The only problem with a civil suit is that it can take years to resolve and if the victim is suing a rapist she may not receive any money—even though the court has awarded her a monetary award. Most criminals do not have assets that can be attached.

There is a difference between the rules of evidence in a criminal and a civil case. A criminal conviction requires proof that can convince a jury *beyond a reasonable doubt*. A civil case requires only a *preponderance of the evidence*. This means that, if the evidence were put on a scale, the heavier side would win. In civil cases, a unanimous vote of the jury is not necessary in order to award judgment in favor of a particular litigant.

A civil trial also, unlike a criminal trial, forces the rapist to take the stand and testify, since in a civil court he is not protected by the Fifth Amendment. So even if he has no assets, the emotional rewards for a victim can make the effort worthwhile. The rapist is forced to take the witness stand and defend himself, with a jury who no longer has to believe beyond a reasonable doubt. A mere scintilla of evidence in favor of the victim is enough.

Lawyers, as a rule, do not require a retaining fee before they take a civil suit. The attorney is normally paid a certain percentage of the damages (the money) collected in a civil case. This percentage, however, may run as high as one half the judgment. Thus, if a woman is awarded $50,000 by the establishment where she was raped, the lawyer might accrue $25,000 of that award.

THE CITIZEN'S ARREST

Few people realize that they have almost the same powers of arrest that an officer of law has, and in some cases a citizen's power exceeds that of an officer's. For a citizen is *not* hampered by the Exclusionary Rule, and any evidence a citizen obtains can be admitted as evidence in a court of law.

To arrest on a misdemeanor, both an officer of the law and a citizen must have witnessed the crime. To arrest on a felony, both the officer and the citizen may make the arrest if they witnessed the felony being committed. And here is where the officer and the citizen differ in their powers: The officer may arrest on probable cause—being told that a felony has been committed and that the person he will arrest is responsible. A citizen may physically *detain* the person who is purported to be responsible, but he does not have the power to arrest the felon. When an arrest is made by an arrest warrant, it is the officer who serves the papers.

A citizen's arrest is made by simply stating to the person whom you are arresting: "This is a citizen's arrest."

If the victim of a rape finds the criminal, she can arrest and turn him over to the law enforcement agency to be put in jail. At the time she brings the rapist to the agency she must sign the complaint against the rapist. Needless to say, a citizen's arrest should never be made by someone who is physically unable to hold the prisoner until he can be turned over to the custody of the law enforcement agent.

5

How to Prepare the Case for Court

A trial is all-out war. Nothing in it is "fair," justice does not prevail, no holds are barred, and no quarter given. Once the victim understands this, she can begin to assemble all of the testimony and physical evidence into a recognizable and easily understood account of horror.

COUNTERACTING THE DEFENSE

Events do not have to be introduced at the trial in the order in which they occurred. Evidence, both testimony and physical, is introduced in the order in which it can best be followed and understood by a jury *that has never* heard the story before. During the preparation of a case for court any "weaknesses" in the case and any possible prejudices of the jurors must be taken into account. These identified areas need to be counter-acted *before* the defense has a chance to bring them up. As an example, consider the following homicide.

During the post-mortem examination it was discovered that the victim's body contained an abnormally high level of drugs—much higher than normal for prescription drugs. The victim was found to be supporting a very expensive drug habit. When word leaked out, the drugs became uppermost in the minds of the community, taking precedence over the murder. Latching onto the community reaction to the news of the drugs, the defense attorney could conceivably have built the murderer's defense on self-defense. Claiming that the victim owed him money for drugs, the defendant could claim that he had tried to collect this money, that the victim had threatened him, and that he had shot the victim in self-defense.

As soon as the amount of money that the victim was spending on drugs became known to the jurors, they would immediately equate that amount with their own finances. Therefore, such a story could be a very plausible explanation—if it was the only one they heard. In truth, the murder victim could well afford the amount of money he was spending on drugs. But of much more importance, the prosecution had the opportunity to prove that the victim started taking drugs only *after* his store had been robbed many times by the murderer, and *after* the victim had received many threatening phone calls from the murderer telling him that he was going to be killed. Only *after* the victim had pleaded with the authorities for help and protection, and been turned down, did the victim resort to drugs to alleviate the tension under which he was living.

How To Speak To The Jury

It is very important that the psychology of the jury members be taken into consideration when points are brought out during the trial. Are the jurors for the most part "conservative" persons? If so, what would most likely be the weakest part of the victim's case? What negative aspect in the minds of the jurors must she overcome? It is far better for the prosecution to be prepared to bring up any "weak points" in its case and overcome them, than to hope that the defense will not introduce them. To approach the subject from a different angle, what can the defense attorney *manufacture* as a "weakness" in the case, and use in the rapist's defense?

Will the defense introduce as a witness the victim's ex-husband who will testify that if his ex-wife did not wear seductive clothing or hang out in bars or other unsavory places she would not have been raped? What has this type of testimony to do with his ex-wife's getting raped? Nothing at all, *except* to plant a negative thought toward the victim into the minds of the jurors. And only one juror must disagree to bring in a verdict resulting in a mistrial. Therefore, if there is a vindictive ex-husband or ex-boyfriend in the life of a victim this possibility must be considered and a plan developed to overcome this type of negative testimony, especially if the rapist is an ex-husband or ex-boyfriend who thinks he still has full sexual privileges.

If some members of the jury, not to mention judges, are prejudiced against women who hitchhike, and the victim has been raped by the man who picked her up, how will the prosecution overcome this prejudice? Certainly not by trying to hide this fact. This is a "weakness" that the defense will play upon loud and long. Therefore, the hitchhiking must be brought out by the prosecutor.

Drug use, in almost any case, invariably results in a negative reaction in some jurors. If the victim had used drugs, whether related in any way to the crime being tried, this is a strike against her. However, drugs taken by the rapist and perhaps having a direct bearing upon the rape itself is often forgiven! Part of our double standard—just as the fact that the victim of rape is on trial as much as the rapist. Most jurors honestly wish to do the best job possible. They also wish to render justice. But they cannot do this without the victim's help.

The only members of a jury who could truly understand the crime of rape are those who have themselves been the victim of a rapist, or have had someone close to them raped. But one of the first questions asked of a prospective juror is whether that person has been a victim of the crime being tried. If the prospective juror has been a victim of such a crime, and often a victim of *any* crime, then that person will be dismissed as a juror.

Therefore, probably none of the members of the jury will have been a victim of rape. Nor will any member of their family or close friends have been victims of rape. And, incredible as it may seem, studies have shown that women jurors are less likely to convict a rapist than are male jurors. Unless the case is one involving a child, it is usually the better tactic to eliminate as many women as possible from the jury. Women seem to be particularly bad jurors in rape cases, trying the victim rather than the defendant. There would appear to be identification with the victim but in a negative manner. In fact, it appears that some woman jurors think convicting on a rape or assault with intent to rape is an admission that it could happen to them. Most male jurors appear to see themselves as protectors of woman and are more willing to convict.

PRESENTING PHYSICAL EVIDENCE

The importance of physical evidence that a jury can touch, hold in their hands, and take back to the jury room with them should never be overlooked. The clothing the victim was wearing, photographs of the scene, fingerprints of the assailant, weapons, and hair samples are all examples of physical evidence which can be introduced in the trial of the rapist.

These pieces of evidence should be carefully arranged for display, rather than be brought to court in evidence envelopes. There are many plastic see-through containers of various sizes and shapes that make excellent display boxes for physical evidence. With a little imagination these can be adapted to all types of evidence. For instance, a broken necklace of the victim may be displayed in a jeweler's box, so that it can be passed to members of the jury without them having to touch the necklace in case it is bloody, etc. Clothing that the victim was wearing may have been tested for blood and acid phosphatase and found positive for both blood and acid phosphatase fluoresce. If the clothing is displayed on a manikin, or on a flat cardboard figure of a woman, then covered with a plastic cover such as a cleaner's bag, it can be dramatically effective to shine a fluorescent Woods light upon the garments and let the jurors see for themselves where the blood and acid phosphatase are on the clothing.

This suggested method of displaying the evidence will be accepted much quicker if the victim secures the containers and helps arrange the exhibit.

Law enforcement officers, in most cases, keep evidence locked securely in evidence rooms, so that no contamination occurs until the evidence has been tested, and so that the evidence will be available for trial. The law enforcement officer will bring the evidence to court.

If a weapon was used and that weapon has not been recovered, it is permissible to obtain a weapon of a similar type and use it for demonstration purposes in the courtroom. If the attack took place in a deserted area, a map and photograph can illustrate this and help establish the fact that the victim had no choice but to submit to the attack.

Photographs of bruises and lacerations on the victim's body, preferably in color, should be used in court. Pictures in sequence, bringing out the extent of the wounds as they develop over several days are very effective bits of evidence. It is not necessary to use all the pictures that have been taken.

In developing the case for court, the statement the victim gave the law enforcement officer at the time she reported the rape, as well as the notes she made about the rape as events returned to her memory, will be the basis of the written text of the trial.

The preparation of the case for court should be done by the prosecutor. However, many prosecutors go into a case "cold turkey." To make sure this does not happen in her case, the victim should provide the prosecutor with her written report of the rape, a list of all the witnesses and what their testimony will be, and a list of all the physical evidence ready to be introduced in court. From her list of witnesses the prosecutor will know who to serve subpoenas for the trial.

Taking her written account of the incident, the rape, as the basis for building the case will help both the victim and the officers involved refresh their memories. Usually many weeks or months pass before the court trial occurs.

Immediately before the trial date, the victim or a law enforcement officer should contact each witness: to let the witness know that they are interested in them and are counting upon their testimony; to go over with the witness what the testimony will be, and how it can be presented positively; to ask if there are any questions the witness would like to ask before the trial; and to give the witness some background into the rapist's past history.

This last note—to give the witness some background into the rapist's past history—may be an entirely new concept for most persons. *Only members of the jury are to be kept in ignorance of the facts of the crime and of the criminal.* And even the members of the jury are allowed to hear of the defendant's past record under previously listed conditions.

Therefore, the more each witness can be brought into the confidence of the victim and the law enforcement officers, the better the witness. A witness, especially a female one, may not wish to say anything against the defendant sitting at the defense table. But if that same witness has background information about the crime, the effect the crime has had upon the victim (possibly victims), the character of the rapist, and the criminal history of the rapist, he or she will be better able to testify convincingly. Either the victim or the law enforcement officer may tell the witness the rapist's background.

If there is a long period of time between the rape investigation and the trial of the rapist, witnesses should be contacted by the victim or a law enforcement agency every few weeks to let them know that they haven't been forgotten. This type of interest on the part of the officer, or department, is an excellent public relations gambit. Victim advocates, Rape Crisis Centers, or the crime prevention officers may be the persons to keep in contact with the witnesses.

Part of the pre-trial preparation consists in getting acquainted with the courtroom. The victim should get to know its physical lay-out—where the witness chair is located in relation to the judge, jury and defendant. This is important, since she will be testifying with the rapist only a few feet away. The prosecutor or law enforcement officer should introduce her to the courtroom. If neither does, she is certainly welcome to take it upon herself to get acquainted with it. She can go while court is in session to observe the workings of the court, or visit the courtroom when it is empty. Many courtrooms are left unlocked while not in use. If the courtroom is locked, she can ask the clerk of the court, whose office is nearby, to allow her to enter. She and her friends might even hold a "dress rehearsal" of the trial in the courtroom before the actual trial begins.

THE VICTIM ON THE STAND

As a rule the victim will be the first witness called. All other witnesses and evidence will be corroborating the victim's testimony. Sometimes there is not much corroborating evidence available in a sexual assault case. Therefore, *even minor details* such as the victim's recollection that there was a red lightbulb in the ceiling of the room to which the defendant took the victim, *if proven*, will provide very important corroborating evidence. One victim—

the Sally of our later case—remembered a blue light underneath the tape deck, that could be seen only from the floor on the passenger side of the car. It is therefore essential that every bit of possible evidence be preserved and gathered immediately after the rape.

In a rape or sex crime, statements by the victim soon after the crime are admissible in court to corroborate the victim's testimony. In legal terminology, this is known as the "spontaneous-declarations exception" of the Res Gestae exception to the Hearsay Rule. They are admissible on the principle that an immediate statement made under the influence of a traumatic event—before the individual has an opportunity to reflect or to fabricate a story—is likely to be reliable. The utterance does not have to be at the exact moment of the event producing the shock.

The victim must objectively examine the crime against her. From the standpoint of a juror, are there any possible questions that need explanations? Or that strike a negative response in the minds of people? Or that the rapist could manufacture as a defense? The question of *consent* will be one of the most important points in the trial. Lack of consent on the part of the victim is one of the elements of the charge of rape. If threat or coersion was used consent is negated.

Consent is in fact a favorite defense of the rapist. He will insist that the victim consented to the act, even though he kidnapped her, or held a knife to her throat or a gun to her head, or threatened her in some other way. Often the jurors will believe the rapist's story, when it was either consent or be badly beaten, cut, or killed if she refused. But the fact that she had no choice often passes right over the heads of the jurors. Therefore, it is necessary for the victim to "paint a picture" in the minds of the jury of just how frightened she was, or of how there was no possibility of escape from this man. The fact that the rapist had a weapon *should* be enough for the jury to see that his victim had no choice.

THE FIRST WITNESS

After the victim testifies, the next person to testify will be the person to whom the victim first told the story of the rape. This could be a friend or relative. Often the first person to hear the story is a law enforcement officer. If the first person to hear the story is a stranger to the victim, that person should have been identified and interviewed as soon as possible to avoid losing his or her evidence.

This witness does not have to quote the exact words used by the victim. In fact, he or she *should not* use the exact words, for the witness may not be able to recall exactly what she said at the time. While going over the case in preparation for the trial, the victim should tell this person to use his or her own words when testifying.

SUBSEQUENT WITNESSES

Although not required, presenting other witnesses in chronological order usually makes the case easier for the jury to follow. Early in the testimony the examining physician should testify. The technician from the crime lab should follow the physician. And nurses who were present should be called to testify at this time. Medical personnel should be prepared to testify by reviewing the history which the victim gave them at the time she was examined after the rape. They can testify regarding the victim's appearance and her mental and emotional state.

Medical personnel should have focused special attention on recording signs of physical violence that confirm the previously collected medical history. Contusions, scratches, abrasions, and lacerations should be described in the record with meticulous detail as to size, coloration, and body location. Grip marks on the upper arms and neck as well as bruises of the thighs are common signs of a struggle with attempts at vaginal penetration. Bite marks should have been noted and photographed, for they may be identifiable to a specific person.

The documentation of breast development in young victims is very important, since young girls who are assaulted may mature into adult-appearing females in the interim between the assault and the trial.

Other witnesses who can be very useful to the prosecution are those who observed struggling, heard screams or any other events that indicate lack of consent on the part of the victim.

The rapist's past victims can testify at the trial, even if he was acquitted, or even if they did not report the rape to a law enforcement agency. Evidence of other crimes is admissible if it casts light on the character of the act under investigation. It can point up motive, intent, absence of mistake, common scheme, identity, or a system or general pattern of criminality. Past victims of the rapist can give excellent and invaluable testimony during the trial, especially in revealing his Modus Operandi.

These victims can be located in several ways. One is through publication of the composite picture of the rapist in papers and on television. Few law enforcement agencies realize how much this can assist them in the apprehension of the rapist. And the service is free of charge. The published picture can include a request to anyone who has information about this man to please call them.

If the law enforcement agency is publicizing the composite, care should be taken that someone on every shift will be assigned to take calls and respond correctly to the telephone message when the primary officer is off duty. More cases than one can dream of have been lost because no one would take a message when it was called in.

The victim also has the privilege of publishing the composite, although she will have to pay for the service. She should work out a procedure to receive calls without endangering herself. Often she can arrange to have the police department phone listed, or the rape-crisis phone. Any crank calls put through to the rape crisis center will be handled routinely by them. Arrangements can also be made with the telephone security officer to secure a special number for calls connected with the picture. Friends of the victim may wish to have their phone number listed, or the victim herself can list her number, if she feels able to cope with the situation.

Some callers may state that the picture looks like a man who raped them—a year ago. The amount of time makes no difference, neither does the fact that they may not have reported the rape. A request to interview the caller-victim can be made while she is still on the phone, with strong reassurance that an interview will be entirely confidential. Her story may ultimately reveal details that only a victim could know. If her rapist *is* the same, her story will closely resemble that of the present victim. This establishes that the rapist is not a first offender, and corroborates the present victim's testimony at trial. Previous victims, given the necessary emotional support, can often be invaluable witnesses in the prosecution of the rapist.

If the victim is fortunate enough to have damaging statements which were made by the defendant, she should use the officer who took them as her final witness. A strong finish is always preferable, especially if no defense is presented.

The defendant does not have to present any evidence in his own behalf, even though the judge declines to grant a direct verdict. The defendant may still feel that there is not sufficient evidence presented by the prosecution to prove him guilty beyond a reasonable doubt. He may rest at this point. The usual procedure, however, is for the defendant to present some evidence, regardless of how weak it may be.

The following pages are an example of a rape case prepared for the prosecutor *by the victim*, with help from a friend. This is a true case. Names and locations have, of course, been changed. Assisted by her husband, she was able to instigate and even conduct most of the investigation. The only physical evidence that the law enforcement agency secured was: 1) the medical evidence that the victim's husband insisted upon and 2) pictures of the welts and scratches left by the belt used to tie her hands and around her neck.

Two days before this case came to court the prosecutor had planned to subpoena only four witnesses—the victim, the physician, the technician who tested the physician's evidence, and the arresting officer. By listening to the victim's account of the rape and her contacts with the various law enforcement agencies, fifteen persons were found who could be witnesses for the prosecution. These persons are listed with the testimony they would be able to give. Also listed is the *physical evidence which should have been gathered!*

The rapist had already spent six months in the county jail waiting for a trial and expecting to be released through a finding of Not Guilty, or to be put on probation immediately after the trial. Had he intended to plead Guilty he would have done so immediately and saved himself the six months wait for a trial. When the rapist saw the large number of witnesses against him he presumed correctly that it was no longer a sure bet to freedom. So he immediately pled Guilty and threw himself on the mercy of the court. This is one of the bonuses of a well-prepared case—the rapist often pleads Guilty, saving the victim the trauma of the trial.

Remember, *no case can be overprepared.*

State vs. John Doe: A Model Case

Charge: <u>Rape</u>   .

Date of Offense: ,

Witnesses and their Testimony:

Mrs. W. D. (SALLY)—Victim. Age 26, Married, living with husband.

1. Driving home from visiting friends, just after midnight. Was forced off road by defendant. Unable to reverse car to escape.
2. Defendant asked to see victim's driver's license. When victim told him that he was no police officer, defendant reached through open vent and unlocked car door.
3. Defendant knocked victim to right, across front seat of car. He pounced on top of victim and started choking her.
4. Victim fought and scratched assailant until she was choked almost unconscious. Victim lost shoes in struggle.
5. Victim agreed to do anything assailant wanted, if he wouldn't kill her.
6. Defendant pulled victim from her car to his car, and shoved her onto floor in front passenger side. Defendant held victim's head down.
7. Defendant drove to deserted area, dragged victim from car, led barefoot victim through path he seemed to know, in an area filled with broken glass and trash—without victim's feet being cut.
8. Defendant ordered victim to take off all of her clothes. Defendant took off all of his clothes except his white low-cut tennis shoes.
9. Defendant then tied victim's hands behind her back with his belt.

10. Defendant threw victim on top of her clothes and raped her repeatedly, both vaginally and anally.
11· Defendant then pulled victim to her knees, released her arms and fastened belt around her neck. While choking her, defendant forced victim to commit fellatio on him. Assault lasted almost two hours.
12· When victim kept pleading not to be killed, and to let her go to pick up her babies, the defendant seemed to become sympathetic. Defendant said he wouldn't hurt victim if she did as he told her.
13· Before leaving area, defendant struck matches to see if he had left any evidence. Found victim's eyeglasses and broken necklace on ground.
14· Defendant ordered victim to dress, dragged victim back to his car. During return trip, victim talked constantly—afraid defendant would kill her. Victim tried to mollify defendant by promising to meet him again.
15· Defendant returned victim to her car. Victim had difficulty starting her car and getting it into reverse. (Victim's purse and car keys were still in her car.)
16· Victim was racing home when she saw two police officers at the square. Victim stopped and screamed, "He tried to kill me! He tried to kill me!" Then she started sobbing.

Police Officer Number One:
1· Can testify to victim's appearance and emotional state at that time.
2· Can testify to the account of the rape the victim told him.
3· Victim was unable to drive further, so he drove victim in her car to her home. But this officer did not believe that victim had been raped! At no time did he take her to police station or doctor, in spite of her hysterics and the fact that it took him thirty minutes to get story.

Officer Number Two:
1· Can verify Officer One's story. Followed victim's car in police car, then picked up Officer Number One at victim's house and left.

Mr. W. D., victim's husband:
1· Was awakened by sobbing victim.
2· Took victim immediately to police station and demanded that victim be taken to hospital for treatment and collection of evidential material.
3· Can testify how he and victim stayed with friends until after defendant was apprehended, for fear defendant would attack again.
4· Can testify how he and victim rode around daily until they located the scene of the assault.
5· While waiting for deputies to arrive at crime scene, victim saw defendant drive slowly by and look at them. Victim recognized defendant as the man who raped her. She pointed to the rapist and thought she was screaming, but no sound came from her. Her husband saw her pointing

and her mouth opening. When defendant suspected he had been recognized, he sped away.

6· How he and victim went to used car dealers to look through books to try to identify defendant's type of automobile.

7· How three days passed before police I.D. man would see them. I.D. officer was unable to make composite. Victim made excellent composite.

8· How victim still too traumatized (after six months) to be left alone.

Female Officer:

1· She was called back to duty to escort victim to hospital.

2· Can testify as to victim's emotional state at this time.

3· Took pictures of scratches on victim.

4· Took written statement from victim concerning the rape assault.

Doctor who examined victim at emergency room:

1· Can testify to victim's emotional state.

2· Give medical testimony concerning examination of victim—bruises, scratches, etc.

3· Testify that I.U.D. was dislocated.

4· Testify to finding live sperm and positive acid phosphatase.

Nurse (Emergency Room):

1· Can testify to victim's emotional state.

Crime Lab Technician:

1· Conducted laboratory examination of evidence—positive.

Used Car Dealer:

1· Can identify victim and her husband as the persons viewing his books to identify assailant's car.

Chief Deputy Sheriff—Officer in charge of investigation.

1· Can identify location of assault and location of defendant's house and place of work.

2· Can identify pictures, if any, taken of crime scene—showing flattened grass, burned matches in flattened area.

3· Arrested defendant at his home. Read defendant his Rights.

4· Can testify to seeing scratches on defendant and identify photos of these wounds.

5· Took statement from defendant denying assault, but admitting being with victim that night.

Deputy Sheriff Number Two: Was with chief deputy when they went to location of assault. Can corroborate chief deputy's testimony about this.

Witness: Any resident of area who heard Sally's car horn the night of rape.

Police Officer Number Three:

1· Took composite picture of defendant and picture of defendant's identified car to all service stations in the area.

2· Received call from sixteen-year-old service station attendant that subject of composite and car fitting description were just in his station. That the car had been newly painted with spray cans and that car paint was still wet. Gave officer the license number of suspect car.

3· Contacted Army base for owner registration and address of owner.

4· Assisted chief deputy in arrest of defendant.

Service station operator:

1· Recognized defendant from composite picture and called police.

2· Paint on car still wet when he came in for gas.

Police Officer Number Four:

1· Assisted Officer Number Three. Can corroborate testimony.

2· Identified blue light under tape-deck in defendant's car. Can only be seen from position victim identified.

Sgt. P.—Army M.P.: Identified auto as belonging to defendant.

Army Sgt. Number Two:

1· Was driving defendant's car when apprehended.

2· Stated that defendant wanted to trade cars because someone was after him (defendant).

3· Identified composite picture as that of defendant and owner of the car he was driving.

Army Pvt.: Friend and roommate of defendant. May have to be declared and questioned as hostile witness:

1· Has stated that defendant told him that he (defendant) had run a girl off the road the night of the rape, but that he hadn't done anything to her.

2· Has also stated that defendant has told him on other occasions that he has run girls off the road.

3· Has stated that he does not trust defendant enough to leave his girlfriend alone with defendant.

Police Officer Number Five: Can identify defendant as man who made complaint to him at police station that a long-haired male had forced him off the road, near the place where victim was forced off road, and that male had beaten the defendant.

Photographs of a crime scene, or any pertinent segment thereof, are as much a form of evidence as a gun used in a murder or a knife in an assault case. Photographs have been described as a particularly satisfactory form of demonstrative evidence because of their power to communicate details to the jury. It is seldom possible for a jury to view a crime scene, and also there are many times when the physical evidence connected with a case cannot be brought into the courtroom because of its size, because of deterioration, or for other reasons, yet being able to view the scene or the physical evidence would materially assist the jury in determining what happened in a case. In these instances a photograph is often substituted for the physical evidence or scene.

There are times when for some reason a photograph could not be taken before alterations were made in a crime scene, or prior to objects being removed, and thereafter an effort is made to reconstruct the scene in order that it may be photographed in as nearly as possible its original state. This kind of photograph has been termed as a "staged" or "posed" photograph. For example, an injured victim may be removed before the scene was photographed or before a gun was picked up from the scene, so someone assumes the position of the body in the crime scene, or the gun is replaced in its original position.

In Sally's case, which is used here as a model, no photographs of the scene were taken at all. The welts and scratches on Sally's neck and arms were photographed at the insistence of her husband. The victim could have gone back to the crime scene which she and her husband had located and could have taken pictures themselves when they realized that the officers were not taking pictures. Even a few days before the trial would not have been too late to take pictures of the crime scene to show the isolated location of the scene. *Victims can contribute a great deal to the investigation, and actually do most of the law enforcement officer's work, if they are aware of the evidence needed, and how to secure it.*

The mere fact that a photograph may be unpleasant or gruesome to look at does not render it inadmissible. Crimes of violence often result in repulsive scenes from which the normal person would withdraw. Photographs of such scenes can be most distasteful, but as long as the photographs are relevant to the issues of the case they are admissible. The fact that a photograph of a mutilated body would inflame the jury more than one less gruesome in nature is not enough to exclude it from evidence. (*People v. Cruz*, 264 Cal. App. 2d 350 1968.)

The mere fact that a photograph may reflect some part of a human body that would not ordinarily be exposed to public view does not render it inadmissible. If there are injuries on portions of a rape victim's body which would not generally be exposed to public view, witnesses should be present during photographing (a nurse, a friend). Seldom is a victim of an attack permitted to display wounds on certain portions of the body in the courtroom. If certain portions of the body do not have to be depicted and are not pertinent to the case, it is suggested that the portion not generally exposed to public view be covered.

Males should be careful in photographing female victims, for the defense counsel can make a most embarrassing issue of a male's photographing a nude female. He may make efforts to impeach the male's testimony. Through ridicule he may divert the whole issue of the injuries.

The following *evidence for the model case* will give the victim some idea of possible photographs to be used in court.

Reconstruct the scene: This photograph is termed a "staged" or "posed" photograph. Always use an asterisk (*) to show staged photographs. *Always* take a photograph of the crime scene *before* any alterations or changes are made, or before any scenes are posed. When the *exact* position of a victim or the *exact* location of a gun is *highly important,* only a photograph taken of the crime scene *before* any alterations or changes were made may reveal the answer to any questions. However, when only *relative* positions or locations of objects in a crime scene are of importance, these photographs can be used without question *provided* someone who saw the original crime scene takes the witness stand to verify the accuracy of the original crime scene. If a posed photograph is taken and if the original object, or an exact duplicate, cannot be used, *something entirely dissimilar* should be used. For example, if there was a gun at the actual crime scene, and another gun of a different make or caliber is placed in the stated scene, the jury may have difficulty in distinguishing the gun about which the testimony is related and the one photographed; whereas if a stick or other marker is used, the jury can quickly determine that it is the *position of the object* and not the object *which is important.*

Models: A woman of the same size as the victim may have to be substituted for the victim when posing certain pictures, to save the victim from further trauma. But *be sure the details are accurate.* In this case a model could pose on her knees with a belt around her neck. Cover the model with a sheet from the armpits down, to show that the victim was naked.

Seminal Fluid and Blood Fluorescence: Be sure to *photograph the fluorescence* around the victim's mouth, neck, clothes and wherever it shows under the Woods light.

Evidence Sheet Written For Prosecutor:

State v. John Doe
Victim: Sally (Mrs. W. D.)
Time: Midnight and After   Weather: Clear.
Date: _____   Moon: One-quarter.

Witness, Sally—victim:
1· Enlarged map of area to show position of cars, buildings, ditch, clay road, crossovers on four-lane, which houses were vacant. This may be drawn on chalkboard, large poster paper, or for overhead projector. Can be photographed for slide projector.
2· *Sally's car posed in area where it was forced off road.
3· *Sally's sandals and purse and car keys in car.
4· Close-up picture of vent window open and door locked—defendant shoved his hand in and unlocked the door and pounced in on top of victim.

5· Picture of car gearshift, with explanation of why she couldn't reverse.

6· *Series* of photos showing thumbprints as they developed on Sally's neck.

7· Inside area of passenger side of front seat of defendant's car, showing tape-deck. Then *posed* picture of victim's position under tape-deck. Then blue light under tape-deck as seen by victim.

8· Overall pictures of area of crime scene, showing clay road, brambles and weeds and broken glass (trash) beside road. Then close-up showing *dim* path through trash. Follow path to matted down grass and burnt matches on grass. Enter burnt matches as evidence.

9· *Posed pictures of Sally's glasses and broken necklace in grass.

10· Sally's eyeglasses (she will be wearing them) and broken necklace.

11· Defendants low-cut tennis shoes, or *posed* picture of like shoes.

12· Defendant's belt (similar belt) used to tie victim.

13· *Posed picture of victim's hands tied behind her back with defendant's belt.

14· Pictures of scratches on victim's wrists.

15· *Posed picture of victim on knees with belt around her neck. (Draped.)

16· Pictures of scratches on victim's neck.

17· Any other pictures of injuries received by victim, bruises, etc.

18· Pictures of fluorescent stains on victim's mouth, neck, etc.

19· Halter victim was wearing when kidnapped, to be *identified*.

20· Overall map showing point of car when she was returned to it, down to the square where they met the two police officers. Also on this map show location of defendant's house and where he worked. Overall picture shows all points are closely connected and that he knew area.

Witness, Police Officer Number One:

1· Can identify the halter top victim was wearing. (It was out of place.)

2· That gearshift in victim's car was difficult to put in reverse.

Witness, Mr. W. D.—victim's husband:

1· Composite picture of defendant made by victim.

2· Pictures secured from used car dealer to identify defendant's car.

Witness, Female Officer: Statement she took from victim regarding the rape.

Witness, Lab Technician: Specimens he examined.

Witness, Police Officer Number Three:

1· Three pictures of car identified by victim as defendant's, that he took to service stations—the year and make of car, plus the year before and after of the same make car.

2· Composite of suspect he took to service stations with car pictures.

3· Picture of defendant's car with fresh paint on it.

Witness, Police Officer Number Four: Identified picture of blue light in defendant's car *after* he assumed position victim was forced into.

Witness, Chief Deputy:

1· Identifies low-cut tennis shoes as those worn by defendant when he was arrested.
2· Statement taken from defendant admitting victim was with him that night.

Witness, Deputy Sheriff Number Two: Picture of defendant's car, newly painted, in front of defendant's home.

Witness, Defendant's roommate: Identifies statement he wrote identifying officers and granting them permission to search home.

6

How to Testify Positively

The victim's testimony is the substance of the trial. If she is unwilling to testify, charges against the rapist are invariably dropped and he is allowed to go free. Because her story is so important, she must be extremely careful of the words she selects and the impression she gives with those words. A successful witness will present the evidence in a composed, coherent manner—and at the same time convey to the jury the violence of the act.

The victim, and every other witness, should have prepared her story long beforehand. Often the defense attorney will leap on her with an accusing question: "Did you or did you not discuss the case before the trial with the prosecutor, and rehearse what you would say?" It is imperative she answer in a way that lets the jury know this is permissible, in fact necessary: "Yes I did. Just as you prepared the rapist for his part in this trial. Will the defense attorney please tell this jury and myself what is wrong in preparing oneself for a court trial?"

The appearance of the victim has a great deal to do with the verdict on the rapist. She should be dressed conservatively, in a dress or suit suitable for a dignified occasion. She should speak clearly and slowly. The jury is trying to place her in a category—is she a "good" woman, or a "bad" woman who got what she deserved? Above all, the victim should show respect for the court—the judge and the officials—whether she feels it or not.

FEAR, ANGER, NERVOUSNESS

The rape victim's emotions during the trial will probably be negative—nervousness, fear, anger, despair, fury, and paranoia. She may be so upset that she is unable to control her emotions. Crying and nervousness on the witness stand appear to be acceptable behavior for a rape victim in the eyes of the jury. But trying to fake this emotion can lose the case for a victim. Jurors can sense when they are being deceived.

The victim should try to control any anger she feels. Anger is easily misunderstood, and jurors can misinterpret the trial as a private vendetta, rather than prosecution of a crime.

USING THE RIGHT TERMINOLOGY

Vulgar language should never be used, even to describe sexual events. There is correct terminology for every act a victim may have been forced to perform. Some of them are listed below:

Adamitism—A form of exhibitionism in which the subject shows himself in the nude.

Annalingus—Sexual pleasure obtained through the use of the mouth on the rectum.

Annilingus—Involves the use of the mouth on the rectum of a male or female.

Bestiality—Sexual act with a beast.

Buggery—Unnatural sexual intercourse.

Cabareting—The underworld name for indulging in abnormal fantasies or daydreams to resolve the sex drive.

Coprolalia—Irresistible impulse to use obscene language.

Coprophagy—The eating of fecal excrement.

Coprophilia—A condition in which a person becomes sexually excited by excretory organs; inordinate interest in feces.

Coprophrasia—A mental disorder characterized by use of obscene language or collection of pornographic literature.

Cunnilingus (also cunnilinctus)—The application of the mouth to the external genitalia of the female.

Exhibitionism—Intentional exposure of sex organs or the nude body under inappropriate conditions.

Fellatio—Stimulation of the penis by friction in the mouth of another person.

Fire-Water Complex—This condition is found as a part of the symptoms occurring in sex pyromaniacs. After lighting a fire there is a period of exhibitionism followed by a desire to urinate.

Flagellation—A psycho-sexual perversion characterized by an intense passion to either whip (sadist) or to be whipped (masochist); whipping, a means of arousing sexual emotions.

Frottage—Sexual gratification obtained by rubbing against another person.

Gerontophilia—The choice of older people of the opposite sex as sexual objects or partners.

Impairing morals—Sexual acts performed by adults upon juveniles or in their presence which would weaken or damage their moral standards.

Incest—Sexual intercourse between closely related persons of the opposite sex, the marriage of whom would be prohibited by law.

Lust Murder—Murder committed in sadistic, brutal, manner: the victim's body usually showing evidence of mutilation, particularly the privates.

Masochism—Erotic or sexual excitement and/or satisfaction from being subjected to pain, whether by oneself or another.

Masturbation—The induction of erection and the obtaining of sexual satisfaction, in either sex, from manual or other artificial mechanical stimulation of the genitals.

Mutual Masturbation—Involves the use of the hands on each others privates to achieve sexual gratification.

Necrophilia—Sexual attraction to corpses.

Paraphilia—A distortion or anomaly of sexuality.

Pederasty—Anal coitus with a boy or young man.

Pederosis—The use of children by adults as sexual objects.

Pedophilia (or paidophilia, or paedophilia)—An adult's sexual attraction to children.

Pervert—One who indulges in unnatural sexual acts or fantasies.

Piquerism—Sexual inclinations to stab, pierce, slash, or cut. Sex gratification is obtained from the shedding of blood, the tearing of flesh, and/or the pain and suffering of the victim.

Psychopathic Personalities—Abnormal persons who suffer from their abnormality and, through the same abnormality, make society suffer.

Rape-Forcible—Sexual intercourse with a woman against her will and consent and despite her resistance.

Sadism—The tendency to associate sexual satisfaction with the infliction of pain on another.

Sado-Masochism—Is a dual deviation in which the individual can secure sexual satisfaction either from the inflicting of pain or from suffering.

Satyriasis—A morbid sex desire in the male.

SPEAKING TO THE JURY

Selection of other words for testifying as a witness can be very important. Certain words can connote negative impressions if used during a rape trial. For example: boyfriend instead of date or escort. When a woman accepts a date with an acquaintance she does not expect that acquaintance to betray her and rape her. When this happens, she should never let the defense attorney refer to the rapist as her boyfriend. She should always correct the attorney when he says *boyfriend* and repeat *date* after him. A boyfriend connotes a close relationship. The rapist is merely an acquaintance who had given her no previous indication of his violence. When they wish, rapists can be very charming.

The defense attorney can insinuate or state that the victim flirted with or acted as a tease toward the rapist. Should the defense attorney accuse her of being a "tease" or a "flirt," as ludicrous as this may be under the circumstances of the rape, the victim needs to set the record straight with more than a *"no"* answer. Although a *"no"* or a *"yes"* answer may be correct, if the witness says yes or no immediately, the attorney may not give the witness time to qualify the statement. Therefore, it is always safer to explain first, to ask a question of the attorney first, then follow it with a yes or no. Such as: "Only a rapist would interpret my politeness as being an invitation to rape. I was not a 'tease'" or "Only a rapist would interpret my fright as flirting. I was not flirting, I was trying to keep the rapist from killing me," or "A rapist can claim anything he wishes to, believing it will be his word against his victim's, as is so often the case. I neither teased nor flirted with the rapist, he pushed himself on me with threats and physical force."

The victim should always refer to the defendant as *the rapist*, and keep that thought before the jury all the time.

Each witness must review her or his testimony with care. How can a negative situation be turned into a positive position for the victim? If there was no physical evidence of a sexual contact, if no sperm nor acid phosphatase has been found, can this be positively presented? Indeed it can, and often the lack of such evidence will carry more weight than its presence. For instance: as soon as the victim is free from the rapist she douches and bathes and washes her hair. Over and over again, trying to wash the rapist out of her system. But she will feel "soiled" for a long, long time. The victim's feelings must be portrayed in such a way as to involve the members of the jury in her trauma.

The victim has destroyed evidence by her bathing and douching. Evidence was not what the victim was thinking of. During the rape she was thinking of how she could keep from getting killed. After the rape she wanted to cleanse herself. And this was the only way she knew how.

During the victim's testimony she has explained to the jury the story of her rape from beginning to end. And she has described vividly how defiled and shocked she was. Now the doctor can be of real help in corroborating the victim's story by explaining to the jury several aspects about the crime of rape that are not universally known. One such fact is that research has shown that about half of the rapists do not have an ejaculation. Or for some other reason, such as condoms, there would be no such evidence had the victim been examined immediately after the rape.

Then the physician tells the jury what he did find, instead of what he did not find. Such as: (1) When he first examined the victim she appeared to be calm and in control of herself. However, this posture was quickly dissolved when the physician started explaining to the victim why he was conducting such a thorough examination, and how the evidence would be examined by technicians in a crime lab to determine if certain elements were present in the samples sent to it. (2) How he has treated the victim for a bladder infection ever since the rape. (3) How he has referred the victim and members of her family to the local mental health department for psychotherapy to help them recover from the after-effects of the crime. (4) That he made a complete examination of the victim and found scratches and bruises over certain parts of her body. That fingernails were broken. That in his experience such physical trauma was compatible with other rape victims he had treated. (5) That this victim suffered great emotional trauma as evidenced by her actions, etc. (6) That although this physician had not examined this patient (the victim) before the rape, in his examination following the rape he found the victim's I.U.D. (and the physician explains an I.U.D. to the jury) had been dislocated, and that it takes a great deal of force to dislocate an I.U.D.

These examples of positive testimony can be used by each witness to illustrate how a witness can examine the testimony she or he will present, and what work would make the testimony presented relay the seriousness of the crime to the jury.

HOW TO ANSWER ANY QUESTION

Each witness should practice speaking directly to the jury. By this I mean answering the questions that are asked by the attorney by facing the jury and speaking directly to them. This will take some practice, for we all have the tendency to look at the person asking the question when we answer. But it is the jury that she is trying to impress. And so it is to the jury that she turns when she is answering. With the judge's permission the expert witness often walks over to the jury box, taking with him the evidence he has examined, in order to explain more thoroughly the tests that he made and how the jurors can see for themselves the outcome of the tests. This can include pictures of bite marks on the victim compared to impressions of the rapist's teeth.

WHEN TO LEAVE THE COURTROOM

Studies have shown that if a victim remains in the courtroom following her testimony she will distract the jury, and this may affect their later decision. One thirteen-year-old victim stayed in the courtroom, and during the remainder of the trial she and her friend giggled together—through sheer nervousness. The jury reasoned that if she could "laugh" during the trial, she must not be very traumatized, and had possibly consented to the rape. They freed the rapist on this one incident alone. Later the rapist bragged of raping the young girl.

Some states routinely use a person who is not an attorney (i.e., a police officer) to act as the prosecutor's "assistant." This person does not have the authority to question witnesses, but he or she does sit at the prosecution's table to keep track of the testimony and make notes of questions to ask or points for the prosecutor to bring out. This is a blessing when the prosecutor comes into his cases cold turkey, and his assistant is the law enforcement officer who worked the case. If arrangements are made beforehand, it may be possible for supporters of the victim to pass notes of worth to the prosecutor for his information. Defense attorneys have been known to hire "jury watchers" to help them select a jury, and to help them interpret how the jurors react to witnesses and prosecution and defense attorneys.

Sometimes prosecutors have very thin skins and must be handled with kid gloves. Every case they win is a "star in their crown" toward getting votes. They should welcome help. There is no disgrace in not knowing a facet of their job, the disgrace is in remaining ignorant in that facet when it is possible to learn.

The victim will be asked by the prosecutor if she sees the rapist in the courtroom, and if so, to please point to him. In answer she should be very firm in her conviction and point to the rapist at the defense table in a very positive manner.

These descriptions of positive testimony can be used by each witness, since they illustrate how a witness can examine the testimony he or she will present and what wording can be used to convey to the jury the seriousness of the crime.

7

The Trauma of Rape

In some ways the trauma of rape is never erased. Years later, even the word "rape" or the glimpse of a familiar face can cause unexplained pain. Rape is a trauma in the same class as murder, kidnapping, and the effects of war. In every case, victims experience the same kind of nightmares, and the same stages of shock, fear, and recovery. Certain traumas are so predictable they have been given names—such as the Buffalo Creek Syndrome. Why do so many people refuse to accept the Rape Trauma Syndrome? Probably because sex is a component of the crime. This causes them to classify it differently.

The Rape Trauma Syndrome is the acute phase and long-term reorganization process that occurs as a result of forcible rape or attempted forcible rape. This syndrome of behavioral, somatic, and psychological reactions is an acute stress reaction to a life-threatening situation.

COMPARISON CASES

Let's compare cases of trauma. It is startling how similar the statements of the victims can be. Take kidnapping. The eminent commentator Paul Harvey, in a newspaper editorial, even called it "routine kidnapping":

"The crime of kidnapping proved such an easy way for Italian terrorists to finance their terrorism that now their modus operandi (MO) is being imitated worldwide.

"Criminals in the United States are discovering it's easier than robbing a bank.

"Jack Evans of Dallas does not drive a yellow Cadillac anymore; he drives a modest smaller car.

"He does not live on a fashionable suburban estate anymore; he lives in a high-security high-rise apartment.

"Because you don't soon recover from an experience such as the one he suffered last February.

"Jack Evans was chairman of a bank. His son was president of that bank. Kidnappers shop for setups like that.

"They kidnapped Mr. Evans Sr. from the parking lot adjacent to his office, drove him at gunpoint to a motel, stripped him and taped his eyes and gagged him and tied him up—striking him if he offered resistance—then the kidnappers negotiated for ransom.

"They got the money. Jack Evans escaped. But he spent four weeks in the hospital getting over the shock—though Evans says he does not expect to ever really get over it.

"In addition to abandoning his luxury car and his country home, Evans resigned his bank directorship and abandoned plans to run for city council.

"Though he might well have been the next mayor of Dallas, Evans says he is unwilling to resume the 'high profile' which makes one a target.

"Capital punishment for kidnappers was abandoned because it was feared the kidnapper would have nothing to lose in killing his victim. It was intended as a protection for kidnap victims.

"But the Jack Evans' kidnappers were sentenced to ten years, may be out in six—and one wonders."

A few more familiar quotes from newspapers: "GUYANA. TROOPS WILL HAVE TROUBLE FORGETTING. Army officers say they expect some of the troops who helped remove the bodies of mass suicide victims in Jonestown, Guyana, last week to suffer emotional scars.

"Officers in the operation were alerting post chaplains, psychologists and counselors to the fact that some of the men may need professional help to get over the nightmarish experience.

"The doctor himself said that he has had problems forgetting his experience in Jonestown.

" 'I can't get my hands clean,' he said. 'I've scrubbed them like I'm going into (surgery), but every once in a while, I catch a whiff and turn, expecting to see another body.' "

"LIFE OF GIRL TAKEN MAN'S LIFE RUINED: WHY, SON OF SAM?

"Since January 30, Johnny has done little but hang out with the rest of the guys. He does not make plans. He is often a little bit drunk.

"January 30th was the day Johnny's girl friend, Christine, was shot to death by Son of Sam, as Johnny sat next to her in his car.

"Johnny is not listed among the killer's victims. From the police point of view, he was lucky. He was physically unhurt.

"But his life has been shattered, just as surely as if one of the killer's bullets had ripped open his head too.

"Sometimes, he says, he daydreams about running over the .44 caliber killer with his car. Or he thinks about the night of January 30 and he thinks what might have happened if he'd turned to look as he started the car, or pulled away from the square without warming up the car, or . . ."

In *The American Journal of Psychiatry*, March 1976, there was a special section devoted to the "Disaster at Buffalo Creek," called *"Family and Character Change at Buffalo Creek."* On February 26, 1972, at 8:00 A.M. on a Saturday morning, an enormous slag dam gave way and unleashed thousands of tons of water and black mud on the Buffalo Creek valley in southern West Virginia. This Appalachian tidal wave destroyed everything in its path, killing 125 people and leaving 4,000 homeless and carrying away human bodies, houses, trailers, cars, and other debris. It expended its force in no more than fifteen minutes at any one point in the eighteen-mile-long valley.

Subsequently, a group of 654 survivors of this disaster from 160 families began a legal action against the company that owned the dam. The suit was settled in July, 1974, for $13.5 million, of which $6 million was for psychological damages.

After the damages were awarded, the legal team then retained a group of experts (headed by psychiatrists) to interview the survivors and assess for the court the psychological impairment they had suffered as a result of the flood. These experts found a definite clinical syndrome, which they called the Buffalo Creek Syndrome, that arose from both the immediate impact of the catastrophe on each individual and the subsequent disruption of the community that affected everyone living there.

During the first days and on into the weeks and months after the disaster, the survivors reported disorganization and sluggishness in thinking and decision making. They complained of having difficulty controlling their emotions. These problems ranged from emotional outbursts to the simple inability to feel anything. Some described transient hallucinations and delusions. Almost all reported anxiety, grief, and despair, with severe sleep disturbances and nightmares. Later, the anxiety was manifested in obsessions and phobias about water, wind, rain, and any other reminder that the disaster could recur. Occasionally these obsessive disturbances coalesced and became a group phenomenon. For instance, the wife of a community leader never slept when he was asleep so that one of them would always be on the alert.

All of the survivors had to confront the loss of a sense of personal invulnerability. The shock was overwhelming and a new outlook took form that reflected a swing from the former sense of invulnerability to pessimism, emptiness, and hopelessness.

The feeling of being a pawn of fate is dehumanizing—people feel without appeal, beyond empathy. When the catastrophe is manmade, dehumanization is magnified. Persons in the helping professions (such as psychiatrists, psychologists, social workers, pastors), and private and public institutions (such as mental health departments, churches, schools) can help victims recover from very stressful situations.

The manifestations of a traumatic neurosis, such as the Buffalo Creek disaster, do not subside with the receding flood waters. *The effects may seem to disappear quickly if one is not alert to the subtle covering-up behavior of the victims of a psychic trauma.*

Let me refer to another article on trauma in the same magazine, *The American Journal of Psychiatry.* Only this article, "Rape Trauma Syndrome," was published in September 1974, eighteen months before "The Buffalo Creek Syndrome." The authors, Dr. Ann Burgess and Dr. Lynda Holmstrom, are pioneers in the research on victims of rape. Theirs is the most definitive work to date on the subject.

Burgess and Holstrom note that when a woman is being sexually assaulted she has to make a choice. Will she give in to the rapist and do whatever the rapist tells her to, or will she fight the rapist even though she may be killed in the fight? Most victims feel that they would rather live than be killed and so choose not to fight the rapist beyond a certain point.

ACUTE PHASE

The rape syndrome is usually a two-phase reaction. The first is the acute phase. In the immediate hours following the rape, the woman may experience an extremely wide range of emotions. The impact of the rape may be so severe as to leave her in a state of shock. When interviewed within a few hours of the rape, the women mainly show two emotional styles; the expressed style, in which feelings of fear, anger, and anxiety are shown through such behavior as crying, sobbing, smiling, restlessness, and tenseness; and the controlled style, in which feelings are masked or hidden and a calm, composed, or subdued affect is seen. A fairly equal number of women show each style.

The expressed style reaction to a rape is the style most persons expect. One victim cried throughout the medical examination, and then throughout the police interview, until a female detective was able to convey to the victim that she understood her feelings.

The controlled style reaction was evidenced in the manner in which one rape victim arrived in the hospital emergency room. The victim quietly waited her turn to be helped, then told why she had come to the emergency room at 3:00 A.M. This victim remained in control of herself throughout the examination and interview, then started sobbing as she reached the hospital door with the friend who had come to take her home.

During the acute phase victims have a difficult time performing even routine necessities of daily living. A young mother may be incapable of taking care of her children. Victims also find that merely washing dishes takes more energy than they have during this acute stage. One mother who was a rape victim said, "I just could not do anything yesterday (the day following the rape). I couldn't even get out of my room. I was able to sleep a bit last night. Today I am trying to do something like housework, but I still just seem to be totally immobilized."

Fear of physical violence and death is the primary feeling described at the time of the rape. Victims state that it is not the rape that is so upsetting as much as the feeling that they would be killed as a result of the assault. One victim stated: "I am really mad. My life is disrupted: every part of it upset. And I have to be grateful I wasn't killed. I thought he would murder me." But victims express a wide gamut of feelings as they begin to deal with the after-effects of the rape. These feelings range from fear, humiliation, and embarrassment to anger, revenge, and self-blame.

The fear of the rapist lasts for months and sometimes years. One victim knew that the rapist was in jail and unable to hurt her himself, but the jail cell windows overlooked the door of the office where the victim worked, so the victim began using the back door of her building to go in or out of her office. At one time this victim was driving her car on a downtown street when she saw the rapist's brother. She became so distraught that she ran a red light in her eagerness to leave the vicinity.

Self-blame is another reaction women describe. For example, a young woman entered her apartment building one afternoon after shopping. As she stopped to take her keys from her purse, she was assaulted in the hallway by a man who then forced his way into her apartment. She fought against him to the point of taking his knife and using it against him and in the process was quite severely beaten, bruised, and raped. Later she said: "I keep wondering maybe if I had done something different when I first saw him that it wouldn't have happened—neither he nor I would be in trouble. Maybe it was my fault. See, that's where I get when I think about it. My father always said whatever a man did to a woman, she provoked it."

PHYSICAL TRAUMA

The second phase of the rape trauma syndrome begins when the woman begins to reorganize her lifestyle. Although the time of onset varies from victim to victim, the second phase often begins about two to three weeks after the attack. Changing residences and jobs, nightmares and phobias, are especially likely during this phase.

During the first several weeks following a rape many of the following acute somatic manifestations are evident:

1. *Physical trauma.* This includes general soreness and bruising from the physical attack in various parts of the body such as the throat, neck, breasts, thighs, legs, and arms. Irritation and trauma to the throat are especially a problem for those women forced to have oral sex.

2. *Skeletal muscle tensions.* Tension headaches and fatigue, as well as sleep pattern disturbances, are common symptoms. Women are either not able to sleep or will fall asleep only to wake and not be able to get back to sleep. Women who have been suddenly awakened from sleep by the assailant frequently find that they will wake each night at the time the attack has occurred. The victim may cry or scream out in her sleep. Victims also describe experiencing a startle reaction—they become edgy and jumpy over minor incidents.

3. *Gastrointestinal irritability.* Women may complain of stomach pains. The appetite may be affected, and the victim may state that she cannot eat, food has no taste, or that she feels nauseated. Victims describe feeling nauseated just thinking of the rape.

4. *Genito-urinary disturbance.* Gynecological symptoms such as vaginal discharge, itching, a burning sensation on urination, are all caused by the germs and bacteria that the rapist introduces into the vaginal area during the rape. One victim, a virgin, developed an infection following the rape that was not treated properly by her physician. The resulting spread of the infection caused the victim to undergo two major operations, and left the victim unable to conceive or bear children. A number of women develop chronic vaginal infections following the rape, due to contamination by the rapist. Rectal bleeding and pain are reported by women who have been forced to have anal sex. Pain in swallowing is a common complaint of women who have been forced to commit fellatio.

MENTAL TRAUMA

All victims experience disorganization in their lifestyle following a rape. They very often change their place of residence in order to ensure safety and to facilitate the victim's ability to function in a normal style. The change of residence is within a relatively short period of time after the rape. There is also a strong need to get away, and some women take trips to other states. Another common response is to turn for support to family members not normally seen daily. Many women make special trips home, which often means traveling to another city.

Victims usually have frightening dreams and nightmares. Women report two types of dreams. In one the victim wishes to do something but then wakes before acting. As time progresses, the second type occurs; the dream material changes somewhat, and frequently the victim reports mastery in the dream—being able to fight off the assailant.

Sandor Rado coined the term "traumatophobia" to define the phobic reaction to a traumatic situation. This phenomenon, which Rado described in war victims, is seen in the rape victim. The phobia develops as a defensive reaction to the circumstances of the rape. The following are the most common phobic reactions:

Fear of indoors, fear of outdoors, fear of being alone, fear of crowds, fear of people behind them (this is common if the woman has been approached suddenly from behind), and sexual fears. Many women experience a crisis in their sexual life as a result of the rape. Their normal sexual style has been disrupted. For women who have had no prior sexual activity, the incident is especially upsetting. For victims who are sexually active, the fear increases when they are confronted by their husband or boyfriend with resuming sexual relations. One victim said: "My boyfriend thought it (the rape) might give me a negative feeling to sex and he wanted to be sure it didn't. That night as soon as we were back in the apartment he wanted to make love. I didn't want sex, especially that night. He also admitted he wanted to know if he would be repulsed by me and unable to."

Let us now consider "acceptable" traumas that are identical to traumas found in victims of rapes:

1. *Son of Sam:* The victim's fiance says, "It pulls me to the cemetery, you know. It's silly, but I talk to myself—to her, I guess—and even if I only stay five minutes, you feel like you're stronger. You feel like you did before for awhile." *A Rape Victim speaks:* "Rape is loss. Like death, it is best treated with a period of mourning and grief. We should develop social ceremonies for rape, rituals, that, like funerals and wakes, would allow the mourners to recover the spirits that the rapist, like death, steals."

2. *The Buffalo Creek Syndrome:* The psychological team found that "All of the survivors had to confront the loss of a sense of personal invulnerability. A feeling of impotent rage over the destruction to life, property, and a way of life. We noted in many people a sense of isolation and feelings of alienation combined with an increased need for vigilance." *A Rape Victim* says: "The basic experience of rape is isolation. Humanity depends on community, and the effect of rape is to destroy simultaneously the sense of community and the sense of person. The effect of rape is the same whether the victim is a young girl, virgin, or older woman. Rape is a crime against the person, not against the hymen. My experience and that of the women I know tells me there is no treatment for rape other than community. Therapy or consciousness-raising can be helpful as long as no 'cure' for a condition or disease is implied."

The social community is the appropriate center for the restoration of spirit, but the rape victim is usually shamed into silence and/or self-imposed isolation. The raped woman often cannot bear to be touched. Isolation is her condition. "Later," said the victim, "I went through the ritual of talking to people. It always seemed as if I were talking through glass or under water. I could never tell my mother; she couldn't bear the pain. Others, it seemed to me, drew away. I could not bear to be alone. But in company I felt abandoned, estranged."

3. *Kidnapping:* Paul Harvey reports about the victim, "They got the money. Jack Evans escaped. But he spent four weeks in the hospital getting over the shock—though Evans says he does not expect to ever really get over it." *A Rape Victim* speaks: "In some ways, rape is never erased. Years later, even the word 'rape' or the shadow of a familiar face can cause unexplained pain."

4. *Son of Sam:* A newspaper reports, "Johnny isn't worried about a meeting with Son of Sam. 'I'm a little edgy still, you know,' he said. 'At night, when I'm driving now, I don't stop for anyone. I'll run 'em right over if they try and stop me.' Sometimes, he says, he daydreams about running over the .44 caliber killer with his car." *A Rape Victim* says: "I felt endangered everywhere. Every noise startled me. Every leaf was camouflage for an assassin. For months a friend of mine described searching the faces on the street as if to ask, 'Are you the one?' Revenge became an obsession."

5. *Guyana:* A physician states, "I can't get my hands clean. I've scrubbed them like I'm going into (surgery) but every once in a while, I catch a whiff and turn, expecting to see another body." *Rape Victims* state: "I don't think I'll ever feel clean again."

8

Avoiding Rape

Susan Brownmiller, in the last chapter of *Against Our Will: Men, Women and Rape*, scorns the use of common sense rules of caution: "While the risk to one potential victim might be slightly diminished (and I doubt this . . .) . . . to accept a special burden of self-protection is to reinforce the concept that women must live and move about in fear and can never expect to achieve the personal freedom, independence and self-assurance of men." I would most vehemently take issue with this. The risk to a potential victim is not *slightly* diminished, if caution is used the risk is greatly diminished.

THE STREET

A woman must constantly be aware of her status as prey. The rapist chooses his victim. First, he looks for a woman who is vulnerable to attack, or for environments that are easily entered and relatively safe. Rapists are particularly good at finding streets, empty laundromats, or theater restrooms that are isolated, but draw unsuspecting victims. After finding a vulnerable target, the rapist proceeds, in essence, to ask his victim, "Can you be intimidated?" If she can, he then threatens her life. He commits his rapes in an environment where he feels safe and comfortable. As he leaves after the rape, the rapist again threatens his victim.

Keep in mind that convicted rapists have admitted to spending hours, even days, devising tricks to catch a woman off-guard. Her best protection is training herself to be in a constant state of caution.

In her book *Rape: The Private Crime, A Social Horror,* Carol V. Horos has listed some excellent precautions to follow:

The Streets—Dangerous Places and Counter-Measures:

Many rapes in the United States either begin or end in the streets. The rapist frequently finds a woman walking the streets, rapes her there or pulls her into a car and drives to another place.

Danger—The probability of being raped increases once the sun goes down.

Counter-Measure—A woman should not take a night walk alone.

Danger—Because of their jobs, some women must walk at night to get to their cars or to wait for public transportation. They are particularly prone to attack.

Counter-Measure 1: If she works at night, a woman could ask a fellow employee if he or she is going in the same direction and will walk with her. Rapists choose the most vulnerable victims and are discouraged by more than one woman. Rapists prefer easy prey and there is strength in numbers.

Counter-Measure 2: Whenever she walks the streets, a woman should stay close to the curb. The most important thing about walking alone is to walk briskly and confidently. Don't look vulnerable, look aggressive and strong.

Counter-Measure 3: A woman shouldn't overburden herself by carrying a multitude of packages or books. She should keep her hands free. The same applies to her purse. She should carry only what is necessary.

Counter-Measure 4: A woman's clothing is a good indication of her chances for fleeing from an attacker. She should wear non-conforming clothes and shoes. Spike heels can only impede escape.

Counter-Measure 5: When she walks, a woman should choose well-lighted streets and avoid streets where there are a lot of bars. If she finds herself on a dark, deserted road, she shouldn't walk on the sidewalk, but in the middle of the street and get off it as soon as she reaches the end of the block.

Counter-Measure 6: She should never stop to give a man directions at night. If he asks her for a match or wants to start a conversation, she should keep walking.

Counter-Measure 7: If a car pulls along side of her she should turn around immediately, walk behind the car and cross quickly to the other side of the street. The same applies if she notices a parked car on the side of the road with the motor running. She should cross the street and leave the area as fast as she can.

Counter-Measure 8: If she is walking and feels she is being followed, she can turn around and look. If she's still suspicious of the person behind her, she can cross the street and walk in the opposite direction. She should head toward the nearest lighted building and tell the person inside that she is being followed, call the police and stay in the building until help arrives.

Counter-Measure 9: If she is being followed in a residential area, she should go to the nearest lighted house and knock on the door. Yell "Fire" not "Rape" or "Help." If she screams "Rape," statistics prove that people within hearing range will run, but not in her direction! Yelling "Fire" produces a kind of no-fault humanitarian reaction by which a person can help in an innocuous way without taking on the responsibility of being involved.

THE CAR

Driving a Car—Precautions to Take: She is somewhat safer in the privacy of her car.

- She should check the back seat and floor of her car before getting in.
- She should lock the car doors and avoid parking on deserted streets and parking lots.
- When she goes to the supermarket or shopping center, she should park as close as she can to the store, particularly at night.
- She must be sure to have the keys ready in her hands, so she won't have to fumble for them in the parking lot.
- If a man approaches the car when she's stopped at a traffic light she should look both ways, keep her hand on the horn and step on the gas. She should not wait for the light to turn green. If she wants to keep a window open, she can roll down the one that is nearest her, not the window opposite her.
- If she thinks a car is following, she should keep her hand on the horn and head toward the nearest police station or business district. She should *not go home, he'll follow her.*
- If it is possible, she should note the make and color of his car and remember it. If she has the opportunity to get a look at the license plate, she can write it down and give it to the police. *The most important thing is to get away from the car.*
- Sometimes, the car behind will flash its headlights off and on. She shouldn't *pull over, but should ignore it and continue driving,* disregarding everything except flashing red or blue lights.
- Anytime she gets into the car, she should make sure there is at least one-quarter of a tank of gas.
- Ideally, house keys should be separated from car keys. If she carries the kind of key chain that has space for the name and address of the owner, she should throw it away; it's dangerous. It's better to lose keys than to have a stranger know where one lives, what's worse, have the key to get into one's home. A woman has to exert the same amount of caution when pulling into her own driveway, and keep the house key ready in her hand.
- With car trouble on the highway, she should pull over to the side of the

road, keep her doors locked and windows up, stay in the car, and look carefully before getting out to raise the hood as a signal for help. If a man stops to help her she should keep the window up—or open to a crack— and ask him to stop at the nearest phone and call for assistance. *But she shouldn't get out of the car or let him try to fix it.*

- If she spots a disabled car, she shouldn't stop, just note the location of the car and stop at the first safe telephone and call the police or highway patrol.
- Waiting for a bus at night is a risky proposition. A woman should avoid waiting on isolated street corners. She should walk to a stop near a business district that is well lit and populated, stand away from the curb until the bus arrives, and once on the bus, sit near the driver. If anyone bothers her she should tell the driver and he or she will drop her off at a safe place.
- Women should never hitchhike; it is the most dangerous means of transportation. She should never—no matter how pitiful, young, or helpless a male hitchhiker appears—pick him up.

THE HOME

Many rapes occur in the home, so it's imperative that a woman take some necessary precautions to lessen her vulnerability.

- For safety's sake, it's essential to know the neighbors. One doesn't have to like them, just know them, exchange telephone numbers and offer to keep an eye on their apartment when they're away. Chances are, they'll do the same for you. One should be extra wary of male neighbors; a high percentage of rapes are committed by the man living next door.
- The second rule of apartment living is never put a first name or use Ms. or Miss on your mailbox.
- Some superintendents ask for a key to your apartment to use in case of fire. If she has close friends in the apartment building, a woman should give a copy of the key and tell the super the third party has it. If he still insists, she can *put the key into an envelope, seal it with wax, and write her name on the wax before it dries. She should check the envelope periodically.*
- *She should never hide her house key.*
- Laundry rooms and elevators are also territories frequented by rapists. When doing laundry, a woman should get in and out of that room as quickly as possible and not forget to lock her front door on the way out.
- Anytime she gets on an elevator, she should stand near the control panel. She shouldn't get on with a strange man. If the man makes a threatening move toward her she should press the *emergency button*. This will set off an alarm that can be heard throughout the building.

- Any dog, no matter how small, is one of the finest protections for the woman who lives alone. It's safer for her and ultimately better for the apartment house if tenants are permitted to own dogs.

THE TELEPHONE

A woman should never list her first name in the telephone book, but give her first two initials, then her last name.

If she receives an obscene phone call, she should just hang up the phone. If the caller does call again, she should tell the phone company. And if he pesters her in the interim, she can tap once on the mouthpiece and say, "Yes, operator, please trace the call now."

Sometimes persons claiming to be poll takers call and ask personal questions. A woman should refuse to give out any personal information. She should condition herself to answer the telephone with a healthy dash of paranoia.

It is also a good idea, if she has the opportunity, to take a course in self-defense or karate. The techniques she learns there will allow her to evaluate her own ability more competently. Most important, *self-defense classes teach women confidence.* A woman who carries herself with confidence, and has knowledge of her own ability to defend herself, can deter a rapist without knowing it. A rapist, like any criminal, often makes his decision to attack in a matter of seconds. During those few seconds he evaluates his victim. A woman with a sense of her own power conveys that sense to the rapist.

Appendix 1

The Rapist Revealed

A. WHY DO MEN RAPE?

Research at Bridgewater divides rapists into four clinical types, according to motivation: (1) *Rape-Aggressive Aim*—when rape is motivated by the displacement of anger from a significant woman (his wife, his mother, etc.) to the victim. The rape occurs as a result of the build-up of irritation and anger within the rapist and is sparked by some event, following which the rapist selects a victim who is a stranger. (2) *Rape-Sexual Aim*—when the rapist is motivated by immature sexual behavior. This type of rapist is less violent and more sexual in aim. The rape is not a breakdown of defenses, as in the rape-aggressive aim, but rather the rape is a defense against strong homosexual wishes. (3) *Rape-Sex-Aggression Diffusion*—is the most dangerous and most rare type of rapist. This rapist does not become aroused without aggression, and his motivation is sexual combined with hatred and aggression toward women. In extreme cases the lust leads to murder. (4) *Impulse Rapist*—is different from the first three types of motivation because it does not involve the interpersonal relationship issue. Most researchers consider the impulse rape an expression of predatory disorder.

From the *victim's* point of view, *the style of attack of the rapist* falls easily into the preceding four motivational categories assigned to rapists by the Bridgewater study.

However, analyze the personality of these rapists. Listen carefully to what the rapist is saying *when he is not trying to impress someone who controls his destiny, someone in authority.* Almost every one of these rapists also fits the category of the predatory disorder of the aggressive antisocial personality—the psychopath, the habitual criminal.

101

In psychological terms, Bridgewater's "Impulse Rapists" may also be called by a variety of names that convey essentially the same meaning: antisocial personality; psychopath; sociopath; acting-out neurotic, aggressive antisocial criminal; hard-core criminal; habitual criminal. By whatever name he is called, *he is not insane;* his personality reveals that he is impatient, impulsive, self-centered, without moral values or loyalties to anyone. *But most important of all, he feels no guilt, and he is incapable of truly loving anyone,* though he may declare otherwise. Criteria for the psychopath: "guiltlessness and lovelessness conspicuously mark the psychopath as different from other men," is found in McCord & McCord's book, *Psychopathy and Delinquency.* The psychopath is a pathological liar. As a liar he has no equal. His ability to lie is unequaled. He lies habitually for the "fun of it."

Most, if not all, previous research has been conducted by persons who controlled the destiny of the rapist in some way. These researchers and treatment personnel also often depended upon the rapist for their own jobs. Therefore, how valid can such research be? It is true that rape is a most frightening, degrading, and humiliating ordeal for victims. *If treatment personnel in a program for sex offenders wish to believe that the emotions of the victims relate in any way to the rapist, or that the rapist was motivated because he hated women,* that he had more trouble with women because he didn't understand them and therefore he wishes to lash out at women in the most humiliating way possible, *then that's what the personnel are going to hear from the rapists.* In fact, most of these inmates know more practical psychology and how to apply it than do many of the professional personnel they deal with. And the criminals have a grand time beating the professionals at their own game!

Through my work and encounters with many victims and their families, I know well the trauma of rape. But I could only speculate on the motivation of the rapist, from information gathered from the sparse literature on the subject. If I talked with a rapist during the investigation of his offense, anything he said to me could be used against him in court. Both the rapist and I knew this. Therefore, I would in a way be able to control the rapist's destiny—which would invalidate anything he might say to me as far as research on his motivation was concerned.

It was not until I was in a unique position to study rapists—informally, with no strings attached and accountable to no one—that I felt my research into the motivation of the rapist could be valid.

One of the first steps in my research was to review inmate records. In one prison I discovered that one in every six inmates had been arrested at some time for some type of sexual offense. Had I not reviewed records I would have missed interviewing many habitual rapists, whose offense on record was not that of rape.

There was a list of questions I wanted to ask each rapist, in order to establish his pattern or style of rape. Questions such as: How do you choose your victims? How do you test your victims to see if they are vulnerable? How do you take your victims under control? How do you threaten your victims? How do you leave your victims, or make your escape? I wanted to obtain sufficient identifiable information to establish this rapist's particular M.O. (Modus Operandi or Method of Operation).

But some of the questions were asked specifically to seek a possible motive. Such questions as: What are your sexual fantasies? At what age did these fantasies begin? How do you feel about women? Do you beat your wife? Do you hate your mother? Did you ever make obscene phone calls? Did you ever steal women's undergarments, and if so, what did you do with or to these garments? How do you justify your rapes?

What I heard through all those hours of interviews proved most revealing. For the most part, what I heard was *not* what I had read in the literature concerning the motives for raping.

CLUES REGARDING THE MOTIVATION OF THE RAPIST

According to the literature, the "impulse rapist" has planned another crime, such as burglary. He breaks into the house with the intent to steal, he finds a female is home, he sees the opportunity to exploit more, and then he proceeds to rape the victim.

But let us look further at the "impulse rapist" who breaks into a house. The primary purpose of most of these men is rape, and the theft is incidental, rather than it being the other way around as many believe. One burglar told me: "You don't even have to look for the money or jewelry before the rape. They'll tell you where the money and valuables are, and offer you anything, hoping you'll take the goods and get out, and not rape or hurt them."

As I listened carefully during my interview with rapists, a pattern began to emerge. Each rapist, in his own words, was revealing his true motive for raping. Each rapist divulged that he raped for the excitement of the "game." The feeling of exhilaration—an emotional high, the thrill of "putting something over on someone"—was his motive. One rapist worded it thus: "Look what I'm getting away with, you fools." Another said, "When I break into a house and rape the girl and burglarize the house I'm really having fun. It's like getting a high on. Why should I work all day when I can do something exciting like rape and burglary?"

Almost the first words spoken to me by one rapist as I interviewed him behind prison walls were, "I don't know why I picked rape. I could have just as easily turned into a bank robber. You know, people rob banks and they get a high on—mentally. It's the same thing. I had sex with the girls—that was the main objective, but the rape wasn't for the sex, it was for the high." One bank robber, in answer to my question of why he robbed banks (bank robbery is a federal crime and brings the F.B.I. into the investigation), answered with, "When you beat the F.B.I. you've beat the best!"

As the thrill of an action diminishes, he extends the risks to extend the high: such as the rapist who operates in an area that he knows is filled with police looking for him; or the burglar who started tickling the feet of his victims to awaken them before he pounced on them and raped them in their own beds.

The rapist picks women and children because they are the easiest and weakest of targets. He picks a time and a place where he feels safe, where he can inflict as much violence upon his victims as he craves. When carefully planned, as most rapes are, the commission of the rape poses very little danger to the rapist.

Rapists commit rapes and sexual batteries upon defenseless victims. In one sense *they lack the courage* to commit a crime during which they themselves might be injured. Because of this, other inmates in prison hold rapists and child molesters in scorn. In the hierarchy of the prison inmates, rapists and child molesters are on the bottom.

Do these criminals wish subconsciously to be caught? Indeed not! They may *say* they are glad they were caught, because they could not stop themselves, or because they needed help. By saying this they get both attention and sympathy, as well as a lighter sentence.

Some rapes *do* occur on "impulse." They are committed by the same personality-disordered criminal, the psychopath/hard-core criminal, that the rapist is. However, this "impulse rapist" is primarily into other types of crimes, such as robbery, forgery, car theft; he rapes because the opportunity is present or because he feels like inflicting violence upon someone and makes the opportunity.

EYMAN'S THEORY OF SPECIALIZED PSYCHOPATHY

Just as in the field of medicine, many psychopaths seem to specialize. And, as in the field of medicine, many psychopaths seem to function as general practitioners before specializing. There are, of course, individuals in both medicine and psychopathy who select their specialities early in life. And there are those who chose to continue in general practice.

Each rapist consistently follows the same style of attack when committing his rapes. His rapes are carefully planned from start to finish. The rapist always controls the situation, whether his method is that of a blitz rape or of a confidence rape. However, while his speciality is rape, the rapist is usually also committing other types of illegal activity or crimes, such as stealing, shoplifting, breaking and entering. The rapist may summon the "courage" to rob, if he feels there is little danger to himself and he can control the situation—such as robbing a convenience store having only one clerk and no customers.

Because these psychopaths have criminal minds, and are always thinking of how to get away with something, or how to put one over on someone, I would prefer to call crimes that do not fit his specialty "crimes of opportunity" rather than "crimes of impulse," for the criminal intent is always in his head. And for the emotional high, the thrill of the moment, the psychopath commits other crimes as the opportunity becomes available—an opportunity that often becomes available through his own endeavors.

In like manner to the rapist, criminals who specialize in other areas of crime, such as robbery, safe-cracking, burglaries—and who plan these specialized crimes with consistent M.O.'s of their own in their specialties—also are committing other crimes outside of their specialized areas. These other crimes, including rape, assault and battery, etc., are also committed for the emotional high, with criminal intent, as the opportunity becomes available, and without a consistent M.O. for these crimes of opportunity.

Psychopaths follow consistent Modus Operandi with their specialized crimes, yet commit other types of crimes seemingly on impulse but actually as the opportunity arises, and without having a consistent Modus Operandi with these crimes of opportunity.

PERSONALITY OF THE PSYCHOPATH/HARD-CORE CRIMINAL

The "antisocial personality" is so different from the psychotic and neurotic, that he must have a special name to distinguish him from these other two. Social scientists can't quite decide on a suitable name for this classification yet. They have his profile down quite well, but they keep changing his name. Some of the names have been superb—"moral imbecile." That's a nice one, but evidently not too many other people thought so, because it never became popular. Psychopath has lasted the longest, is still in use today and is a favorite. However, when one hears a word with *psycho* in it, people immediately think of someone insane. A psychopath is *not insane.*

In 1952, the American Psychiatric Association replaced "psychopathic" with "sociopathic." In terms of official psychiatric nomenclature, the term psychopath could be characterized as "sociopathic personality disturbance, antisocial reaction." With the term sociopath, people didn't immediately think of insanity. This personality seems to be at war with society.

Again, in 1968, the term used to designate a psychopath was changed by the American Psychiatric Association to that of "antisocial personality."

There is also a character disorder that is called an "acting-out neurotic," who acts and reacts almost exactly like the psychopath. There is such a fine line between these two personalities that even some psychiatrists have trouble differentiating between them. But you're just as dead if you've been murdered by an acting-out neurotic as by a psychopath, by a fourteen-year-old as by a forty-year-old.

Now comes a new name for this antisocial personality who has ended up in prison—he's called a hard-core criminal or habitual criminal. In 1960, a seventeen-year, federally financed, three-volume study of this personality was begun. It is called *The Criminal Personality*, by Yochelson and Samenow. This three-volume study is summarized in the May 1978 issue of the *Reader's Digest*, "The Criminal Mind: A Startling New Look," by Eugene H. Methvin, pp. 120-24. Methvin states, "The startling findings seem to point to a grim, distasteful conclusion: 'nothing works' in rehabilitating most of these hard-core Charlies; for the immediate future we must be prepared to imprison them permanently."

Actually, this is not "a startling new look" nor "a startling finding." The syndrome of the psychopath/hard-core criminal was thoroughly discussed in an extremely interesting and easy-to-read and understand book which was published in 1956, called *Psychopathy and Delinquency*, by McCord and McCord. This book was revised and abridged by the authors and published in paperback in 1964 under the title *The Psychopath, An Essay on the Criminal Mind*. Both of these studies arrive at the same conclusion; that for all *practical* purposes there is no cure for this type of personality—the psychopath/hard-core criminal—at this time.

It is important to become accustomed to the term psychopath. I shall use the terms psychopath hard-core criminal often, as well as other designations for this character disorder—sociopath, antisocial personality, psychopath, hard-core criminal, career criminal, rapist. *But a word of caution:* far from all psychopaths are in prison. Many are extremely dangerous and will kill without provocation. Others stay just on the periphery of crime, but cause heartache and misery to those who must live or work with them.

PSYCHOTICS, NEUROTICS, AND PSYCHOPATHS

Let's start with personality traits that more people are already familiar with. Professionals have classified the *insane* for us; they have agreed to call them *psychotics*. They have also defined a psychotic as one who is out of touch with reality. There are several different types of psychotics: the schizophrenic—the person commonly called a "split personality," although this is a misnomer. The paranoid psychotic believes that everyone is against him. We all feel this way sometimes, but to a much lesser degree than does the true paranoiac. The manic-depressive psychotic is sometimes supercharged and never seems to tire or need sleep, and at other times is in such a deep depression that he hardly functions. In this depressive state he is often prone to suicide. These labels simply describe some of the different types of mental illnesses diagnosed as psychotic. Drug therapy is very useful in treating many psychotic illnesses.

How well psychotics can function makes the difference in whether they are allowed to walk around in the free world or are locked away in an institution. If they can take care of themselves, or have someone who will take care of them, and if they are not a danger to anyone or to themselves, then they are allowed to live free. In fact, if psychotics are wealthy enough, they aren't even called crazy—they're called eccentric.

The great mass of "normal" people are also classified—we're called neurotics. Some of us are more neurotic than others, and some of us are so neurotic that we fall across that fine dividing line between neurosis and psychosis, and lose contact with reality. Both neurotics and psychotics feel guilt. Sometimes people feel so guilty that they go crazy, quite literally. But most of us just have consciences that make us feel uncomfortable, maybe because we did something wrong, or were ashamed for something we did or didn't do. Because we have a conscience we can empathize with these people. We understand, as nearly as possible, how they feel.

It is this very conscience of ours, our feelings of guilt, that makes it so difficult for us to understand someone who feels no guilt. *The two glaring personality deficiencies that distinguish the psychopath/hard-core criminal from all other types of deviant behavior are his guiltlessness and his lovelessness.* As long as he is doing what he wants to do that's all that matters to him. And if someone or something blocks his way he will often explode in anger.

The psychopath/hard-core criminal is totally incapable of feeling empathy with anyone. The Indian prayer, "Let me not judge a man until I have walked a mile in his moccasins," is completely beyond the comprehension of the psychopath/hard-core criminal. This antisocial personality cannot put himself in anyone else's place and feel as they do. Nor does he care to do so.

This antisocial personality will cheat, steal, lie, rape, murder, kidnap, embezzle and commit forgery and not feel the least bit of guilt about his behavior. He will not accept responsibility for his acts—even when caught in the act. He can always explain how it was someone else's fault. Or how someone else made him do it. The rapist will say, "She asked for it." The murderer may say, "He tried to kill me. I had to defend myself." He is thoroughly irresponsible in all aspects of his life.

This, I believe, is where a "normal" person has the most difficulty in understanding the personality of a psychopath/hard-core criminal. How can *anyone* do the things that psychopath/hard-core criminals do unless they are "sick"? Unless they are "crazy," "insane"? They may be abnormal, but they are *not* "sick" and they are *not* insane. They can do these things because they feel no guilt. They have no conscience to hurt them or to slow them down. With no feelings of guilt, a psychopath also beats the polygraph (lie detector).

We might draw an analogy between a psychopath/hard-core criminal and a man who has had a few drinks to get up his "courage." The alcohol doesn't give a person "courage" or "make him mean." The alcohol takes away a person's inhibitions, dulls his conscience, masks his moral defenses, and releases the raw personality that his inhibitions, his conscience has kept in check. And so, under the influence of alcohol, a person may act and react in a totally different manner than he will when he is cold sober, or in control of his senses. But a psychopath/hard-core criminal doesn't have to be under the influence of alcohol to lower or get rid of his inhibitions, his defenses, for he has few inhibitions to begin with. He has none of this automatic self-checking apparatus that our conscience functions and controls for us, because *essentially he has no conscience.*

The psychopath/hard-core criminal can *say* that he is sorry, but he doesn't *feel* sorry. He's sorry he got caught, not sorry he committed the act. But he can be a very convincing liar. He can say all the right things. And you may end up forgiving him or taking the blame yourself! This personality disorder is often not evident on short acquaintance. But if one has been around him for some time and analyzes his behavior, it will be apparent that everything he does—if it makes trouble—is someone else's fault. The psychopath/hard-core criminal's personality can often be recognized through his F.B.I. criminal record. His F.B.I. record may show a number of *different types of crimes* that he has been arrested for.

Notice him as the defendant in a courtroom. It is as though he were not the man on trial. He can act, and is, totally oblivious of the seriousness of the situation. It is as though he were a detached onlooker, completely devoid of any guilt in the proceedings. His behavior in the courtroom, his calm, cool detached air is one of the giveaways to the psychopathic/hard-core criminal's personality. If he displays emotion, such as anger, it is at the so-called injustices being done to him in the courtroom. Not the "normal" emotion of guilt, or sorrow—for himself and the injuries he has caused his victims or the shame he has caused his family.

Which brings up the other unique trait of the psychopath/hard-core criminal. Besides his inability to feel guilt, he is also unable to love. Guilt-lessness and lovelessness are the two critical traits that set this personality disorder apart from all others.

We are *not* talking now of a person so inhibited that he is unable to *express or show* love. There are many people unable to outwardly display affection, but they are able to convey love in many different ways. But the psychopath/hard-core criminal is unable to either give or receive genuine love. His affectional relationships are always shallow and self-serving. However, he may be able to *sound* as though he truly loves. There is little stability in his relationships. Promiscuity is the rule. Close friendship and allegiance to anyone or anything is beyond a psychopath's capabilities.

Other unsavory characteristics of the psychopath/hard-core criminal include his callousness and insensitivity to other persons. Other persons are important to him only insofar as he can use them to his own selfish purposes. He is greedy and demanding. He seeks only his own pleasure. Standards of ordinary decency mean nothing to him. He is interested in immediate fulfillment of his own wishes and needs, and will attempt to satisfy them without regard for others. Because of this irrational desire for immediate gratification, he rarely learns from experience. He will continue to behave in a manner that is destructive to both himself and to others, because he has developed no self-control to modify his behavior and he has no pangs of conscience to bother him.

Rarely does the psychopath/hard-core criminal hold onto a job for long, although he may be quite skilled in his profession. He soon tires of a routine job. As a result he may quit, participate in flagrantly dishonest and unethical practices, abrogate responsibility, and behave in other ways that result in an unstable and shifting employment record.

Sex for a psychopath/hard-core criminal is just that. No love involved, only physical contact—sometimes. For the psychopath/hard-core criminal can be heterosexual, homosexual, auto-sexual. In the words of that eminent criminologist, Dr. George G. Killinger, "A psychopath would have sex with a snake if he could hold it still!"

It is necessary to remember that psychopathic characteristics exist in varying degrees in different individuals. Some criminals are more psychopathic than others; and not all criminals are psychopaths. In like manner, not all psychopaths are convicted criminals. For example, there is the social parasite who stays just within the bounds of the law, or the moral hypocrite who successfully evades legal actions.

The psychopath can very cleverly display an exterior charm and manipulate people within his environment. Often his dangerous traits are not readily apparent. For all practical purposes, once the defect is created it cannot be changed. The psychopath/hard-core criminal does not have the genuine sense of self-dissatisfaction needed to effect a personality change. As far as he is concerned, there is nothing wrong in his own personality that needs changing.

WHAT CAN BE DONE?

Assuming that most rapists are psychopaths, and also that hard-core criminals of other specialties are also psychopaths, what then can be done for or with them?

Psychiatrists really do not know the cause of sexual dysfunction or sexual deviancy. Nor, if they get enough people together, can they even agree as to what is normal and what is abnormal in sexual behavior. The term "sexual offender" itself is a legal term. It is not a medical, psychiatric, nor psychological term.

Psychiatrists are unreliable in predicting dangerousness. Some people may be dangerous and not mentally ill, and others may be severely mentally ill but not violent or dangerous. A psychiatrist *may* be in a position to predict future violent behavior *if* his patient has a history of past violent behavior under certain conditions or circumstances that may likely be repeated in the future.

Psychopaths are *not* mentally ill. Nor are rapists who are psychopaths mentally ill. It follows then that they cannot be treated; for treatment really means amelioration of symptoms and possibly cure. Therefore, *sex-offender programs cannot be and are not effective.*

In brief, "The Criminal Mind: A Startling New Look," published in the May 1978 issue of the *Reader's Digest,* (as well as McCord and McCord's *The Psychopath),* provide an answer: "The startling findings seem to point to a grim, distasteful conclusion: 'nothing works' in rehabilitating most of these hard-core Charlies: for the immediate future we must be prepared to imprison them permanently. But a more helpful, exciting conclusion also emerges; we can make a huge reduction in crime by early identification and incarceration of a relatively small proportion of offenders."

If men rape, as they say they do, for the emotional high it gives them; and if rapists are habitual criminals, as my research indicates, then there already exists a way in many states to deal with this criminal. By using Habitual Felon Laws (the "three-time loser" laws) that have long been on the statutes of many states, we already have the necessary laws to permanently incarcerate rapists and other hard-core criminals.

B. INTERVIEWS WITH RAPISTS

MIKE

The Police Report

"*Circumstances of the Offense:* On the afternoon of November 21, 1963, while working for yard spray company the subject was driving through the half-rural neighborhood of Hampton Road in the southern part of the county, when he spotted a little girl walking along by herself. She was ten years old and lived with her parents at the above address. The subject stopped the truck and called her over to him. When she came he got out of the truck and struck her a severe blow above the head with a tire iron. He then threw her on the front seat of the truck and getting in beside her drove off unnoticed. Coming to a deserted area off Hampton Road, at about 148th Street, he parked the truck in a rock pit and struck her again on the head with a tire iron to make sure she was dead. He then pulled down her clothes and sexually molested her by forcing his fingers into her vagina. After masturbating into her clothes, he cast the body aside and left undetected. He drove to a secluded spot on the edge of a lake where he washed the blood of the victim out of the truck and then he returned to work.

"The sheriff's department launched an all-out search for the child when she was first reported missing by her parents, on November 21, 1963. On November 21, 1963, police, citizens, and 120 army personnel walking arm in arm over marked-off areas in the neighborhood came upon the dead body of the child. She was laying face down on a rock pile and her clothes were pulled down around her ankles.

"An autopsy revealed contused lacerations to the scalp, compound comminuted skull fractures, depressed comminuted skull fractures, marked cerebral contusions of the broad ligaments of the uterus by lateral, and postmortem decomposition consistent with about forty-eight-hours duration.

"At the scene of the crime police investigators lifted a tire print, and an expert gave them a description of the truck to which it belonged. Such a truck was found to be owned by the spray company that the subject worked for. And further investigation revealed that on November 15, 1963, a man in a truck bearing the same company name had attempted to pick up a seven-year-old girl in the same general neighborhood. And the parents had made a complaint to the police.

"The owner of the company was questioned and he said that on June 15, 1963, some clients had made a complaint to him that one of his employees had made some improper remarks to their fifteen-year-old daughter, while spraying the lawn. This employee was determined to be the subject and was called down to the sheriff's office for questioning. He denied the offense and he was released. But it was determined that he was a convicted felon who had not made criminal registration and he was charged and fingerprinted accordingly.

"The investigation continued and there was an especial urgency because on October 6, 1963, a skeleton was found by a hunter in a wooded area off Hampton Road at about 150th Street. And these remains were determined to be a nineteen-year-old, mentally retarded female, who had been missing from her home since August. Her skull had been fractured and there was evidence of sexual foul play, and the police were certain the same person was responsible for both crimes.

"On December 27, 1963, police investigators matched a fingerprint of the subject (the murderer) with a bloody fingerprint found on the clothing of the second victim (the ten-year-old girl).

"He (the murderer) was again taken into custody, and while awaiting the taking of a polygram (lie-detector) he was left unattended. At which time he bit himself severely on the top of his right hand and stabbed a screwdriver into his arm. He was charged with disorderly conduct and attempted suicide and he was transferred to the hospital for medical care. The following day the subject was visited in his hospital room by a detective disguised as a psychiatrist." (Author's note: The law requiring law enforcement officers to read a suspect his rights, called the Miranda Decision, did not go into effect until 1967.) "And this detective obtained a confession to both murders from the subject (the murderer). He was promptly charged with first degree murder and he has been confined in the county jail since."

"Subject's (the murderer's) statement on first murder (nineteen-year-old girl): The subject readily admits his guilt. He said that one day in August he was at the company shop located at the aforementioned address, when he saw the victim hitchhiking. He got into his truck and picked her up. She said that she was trying to get down to the nearby air force base, because she had a date with three airmen. The subject said that he would take her down there but that he had a little work to do first. While driving along they began talking about sexual subjects and when he stopped the truck near where the body was found she consented to all kinds of sexual misbehavior with him. The subject said that then all of a sudden before he knew what he was doing he was beating her over the head with a tire iron. Then he felt much better and masturbated over the body. He then threw the body into a thicket and left. On at least four occasions before the body was discovered the subject returned to the scene of the crime and studied the progress of the decomposition of the body. Each time he masturbated over the body, and he also tried to pull the head off and an arm, but he was unsuccessful. He was very unhappy when he learned that the body had been discovered.

"*In regards to the second offense,* the subject said that he was driving along when he noticed the little girl (ten-year-old victim) and called her over to the truck. She said that she was going to visit her horse and the next thing he knew he had struck her a severe blow on the head with a tire iron. He threw her body into the truck and drove off. He was very surprised that no one saw him because he struck her in broad daylight in front of many houses in the neighborhood. Subject then said that he drove to a secluded spot where he struck the victim again until he was certain she was dead. He then molested her by tearing at her vagina with his fingers. After masturbating over the body and into her clothes he left. After washing the blood out of the truck he returned to work. The subject said that he was very unhappy when the body of his second victim was discovered so quickly. He said that there were so many things that he wished to do with the bodies."

"*Mental Health:* The subject was examined by *four psychiatrists,* as ordered by the court, and all brought forth a diagnosis that though *the subject was not insane* he was suffering from a severe *sociopathic personality disorder.* He gives the impression of *conscientiously contriving to act in a disorganized manner.* He can be classified as a sociopathic personality disturbance with characteristics of deviant sexuality and asocial and amoral trends. We consider him to be mentally competent, both at the time of the alleged crime and at the present time."

"*Employment Record:* This subject's employment record is very diversified and spans a long number of jobs of brief duration."

"*Community Attitude: The state's attorney* says that he does not think the subject should ever be released from custody. And to insure this he is filing a detainer against the subject charging him with the murder of the nineteen-year-old girl."

"*The police captain* said that he feels that the subject is pretending to be mentally ill in an effort to escape the electric chair. He feels that regarding the present offense the subject turned his attention to little girls and killed them after sexually molesting them so that they would not be able to identify him. He feels that the subject should go to the electric chair.

"*A second police captain* states that the victim's mother was a pretty stable woman who held no intense animosity toward the subject, but felt that in the best interest of society the subject should be done away with. The father of the other victim sent a six-page telegram (saying) 'and send this animal to the electric chair' after he heard he might get a life sentence.

"*Subject's (Murderer) landlord and neighbor* said that he found the subject to be such a kind and friendly man that it is hard for him to believe that the subject could be guilty of such a crime."

THE MURDERER'S VERSION

This murderer tells so many lies that it is hard to separate the truth from the lie. However, the stories he tells about the murders, fifteen years after first telling them to police officers, remain essentially the same as the ones he told at the time of the murders. So we can learn about this man from his description of his feelings at the time of the murders up to the present day.

The murder of the nineteen-year-old; in August 1963: "I was driving down the road and this hitchhiker flagged me down. She got in the truck and she asked me where I was going. And I was going down part way toward where she wanted to go, because I was going to spray down that way. We were riding along and I turned around and I said, 'You don't mind if we drive off and stop for a little while and let me talk with you?' And she said, 'No.' So we went on and turned around and turned off the road into the woods. And I stopped and we got out of the truck, and you could tell by her speech pattern that she wasn't quite right. And between you and me, it stimulated me. Sexually. And I asked her, 'Do you mind if we go out here and have some sex?'

"So we went out there and I stopped. And I told her to take her clothes off. So she just turned around and dropped her shorts and everything. And she was a developed woman, she wasn't no girl. She was nineteen. And we laid down there and I went on and had sex with her. And just about the time I was getting ready to climax she started crying. And I just went ahead and kept on until I did climax. So I got up and she put her clothes on and she was real talkative. She talked about everything in the book. So I got up and walked on back to the truck, and she came over there by the truck. And then she started talking about her mama and her daddy and policemen and everything and I actually got a little scared. And again, that bar was on the side of the truck. And I just struck her with it. I struck her hard. When I hit her it knocked her feet out from under her and she turned a half flip. So I had to have a tremendous force behind it for her to do that. And I took and put her back in the woods and ripped off her clothes, and I drove off. I just left her laying out in the open.

"And at a later date I came back and I walked out and the body was deteriorating. She was laying there, and she hadn't started to deteriorate or anything. There were some blowflies around her face. And I felt her. I reached down and touched her skin. It was tight, but it was cold. In fact it was cool like it had just come out of the icebox. And I just stood over her and masturbated while I looked at her.

"And one day I was walking home and I got caught in a rainstorm, and I took my wallet and stuff out and put it in this here mailbox on the side of the road. Then I came back and later on picked the wallet up. Well one time, the second or third time I was out there where she was at when she was deteriorating pretty bad, cheek bones are starting to show up from deterioration, worms eating her. And for some reason I just thought it would be funny to put her head in this mailbox. And I reached down and I started to twist it. When I did the skin on her hair came off in my hands and I quit. It stunk and was all over my hands. So I went and washed them in a ditch and I left.

"When I came back she had turned tan. Tannish yellow. And her whole body, like we have creases, all of this was solid round. Her legs, you couldn't tell where the knee cap was at. And the skin was plastic looking. And the skin was tight like an aluminum soft drink can—that's the way her skin was. This can felt just like her skin, but her skin was warm. You could press on the skin and it was soft but firm, and it came back out. Her tongue was completely round and dark grey and came out. Her mouth was wide open. Lots of flies and maggots around her mouth and tongue and around her right cheek where the holes were. And a lot of maggots down around her vagina.

"I went back about every three or four days to look at her, then every week. Once I drove out to the place with my wife—I mean the woman I was living with—and my children and I was planning to say I had discovered her then, but I decided just to masturbate over her at that time, so I came back to the car and we drove away. She was just skin and bones the last time I saw her."

The murder of the ten-year-old; in November 1963: "This second girl, I was driving along and I seen her walking along the road and I just stopped and got out of the truck and walked around and asked her where she was going and she said she was going to see her horse, and I just reached up there and struck her with the tire iron. And there's people walking up and down the street, which surprised me because nobody paid any attention, because I didn't hide it.

"I drove approximately a block from the area, and I stopped the truck and I grabbed her and I threw her from the truck. And she fell on the ground. And I walked over and put my foot on her and reached down and ripped her pants off of her. Shorts, or skirt, I don't even remember which. Skirt I think. And like I say, she only had one or two hairs on her and she was too small, as far as sex is concerned. And I want to say my killings wasn't related to sex, but I can't. When I seen she was too young, she just had one or two hairs, I shut my eyes and I visualized sexual acts with a woman. And when I got through I reached down and I grabbed her, I grabbed her by the leg and she slipped and I turned around and I ran my finger—which is what ended up getting me the electric, uh, what got me the life sentence. I rammed my hand, I rammed it intentionally now. Don't get me wrong, I'm not saying I didn't do it on purpose. I rammed my finger up in her vagina, and grabbed her by the arm, and slung her off to one side. Then I picked up her clothes and wiped the blood off my hand and slung the clothes over on her. And that was it. As far as sexually molesting her that's as far as I went. I'm not trying to make it lighter than what it is. But, then I left.

"And the funny part, what struck me now in relationship to what happened then—I knew I was guilty, I knew I would get it, but I couldn't associate myself with the act itself. I could tell you all the details about it, the whole works, but I couldn't associate any, uh, uh, myself with it. Now I'm not trying to say a split personality or nothing of that stuff, this is what happened.

"And people ask what made me do it, what was I thinking about when I reached over and grabbed the tire iron. Let me see if I can describe it. Have you ever been in a car and went up over a hill, and felt your stomach? Well, multiply that hundreds of times over. I hate to say it, but this was the first time that I killed for sexual motivation or a sexual drive if you want to call it that.

"I want to tell you that I wasn't planning on striking her, but I'd be lying. But I can't really honestly say I'm going to get out and walk over and pick up this bar and strike this little girl and kill her. *I knew it was coming, and yet—it wasn't intentional.* Let me explain, it was like this. I brought these pictures over intentionally for a purpose. When I drove by her and pulled over and stopped, it was the same as me bringing these pictures over to show you, that I was going to kill her. But that section of it wasn't planned. It just, it was just there, it was just going to happen.

"I just struck her with the tire iron. It's one of these things I used to be able to do, I could almost let myself *not* think. I can act and not associate thought with it. In other words, it was just like reaching over here real quick and tearing these pictures in half.

"I was able somehow to be able to kill her and drive off and not associate myself with the actual crime. I knew I did it, I'm not saying I didn't know it. I'm not saying I was a complete innocent. As far as not realizing I did it. It's like this: in the Vietnam war thousands of people got killed. Well I'm sorry. It doesn't pertain to me. There was a bad wreck on the highway up here, seven people got killed the other night in a truck crash, *but*—there was a girl killed in my town. And yet, I didn't associate the two killings with me. But yet I knew the car, I knew the truck, I knew the place where it happened, but it wasn't me.

"What was strange about it was I would do this and once I got away from the area it was no more than if I had been driving down the road and had seen an accident and if I happened to be driving back down the road again it reminded me of the accident. It was the same thing with the girl (the nineteen-year-old victim).

"Once I did it, I never thought about it in the daytime, while I was working or anything. It was just on my way home and I was driving by and would get close to the area, it dawned on me and I'd just drive off over there. And it would seem like something like this would be real conscious of, don't you know, but I didn't pay no more attention to it. I just didn't think of it until I was there at the area where this girl was at, which is on the way home. And I'd stop by.

"Several times I've been in the area and haven't thought about it."

This multiple-murderer says, "I have never raped a girl in my life. I've thought about it. I've fantasized about it. But I've never participated in it. Even in here (prison) today when I encounter a sex offender I have to mentally control my emotions for rejecting that man. I can't never completely accept him. All my life it even upsets me to see somebody strike a kid, spank them. Now if you want to get me up tight, let the old lady start raising hell with the kids and wanting to spank one of them. They'd run to daddy."

Questions from the interviewer: "Did you have an opportunity to kill again?" *Answer:* "You can make your own opportunity. If you're going to kill you get the victim in an isolated area, so no one will hear the screaming. And if you're going to break into a house it's always easier to knock on the door and let them open it for you, then walk right in."

Question: "Did your wife ever suspect that you were guilty of any of this (the murders)?" *Answer:* "I don't think so, in fact, I didn't feel guilty about them or upset. Because I came home and the newspapers were full of it, and I told her not to let any of the kids out away from the house. Again let me say, *I just never place myself in the category of being a perverted type of person of this type of caliber.* It's hard for me to believe what I have did—I know I did it. Now I'm not saying that I don't realize it, but when I get to talking about it, I feel relaxed now, when I first start talking about it, I feel guilty, I feel—I finally started feeling remorse for it. For a long time I couldn't even feel remorse and that bothered me a lot, because I couldn't visualize a man committing this type of crime and not having no remorse about it. *I felt sorry about the turmoil my family went through or maybe her family went through. As far as her as an individual victim of my actions it was hard to feel any sorrow for her.*

"After the newspapers blew up this murder they questioned me about murders all over the United States, places where I'd been. That was all they could pin on me. Of course I denied them. When I was in jail I laid up there and I could sit there and I could tell a story that would be basically part truth and part lies, and I could say it with all the conviction in the world, and I could stand back and say that's a lie."

Question: "You fantasized in Max (maximum security prison) about having sex with the first girl that you killed?" *Answer:* "Yes. She was what I consider a very, very—she was just inactive, she just laid there. I could have taken the leg off the table, an arm off of the chair, back off a settee, and got about as much movement out of it. But it was the last normal sex act I had, prior to coming to prison. And I couldn't remember having sex with the girl I was living with, so I did fantasize having her out there. But as far as the killing part, I left that out of my fantasies.

"My wife—the woman I was living with—and me, we were inseparable, in fact I enjoyed having her around. *And the worse thing about it was when I come to prison and I was laying up in Max the most worse thing, even worse than the killings was the fact that I was losing—or I had let my kids and her down. That was the most horrible feeling in my life, man. I wished I could have had them with me and could light a case of dynamite and blow us all up together. And I mean, boy it was horrible. To lose them, you know.*"

For the Record:

"This man was charged with first degree murder in that on November 21, 1963, he did kill and murder (the ten-year-old) by striking and beating her about the head with a blunt instrument. On February 24, 1964, the subject was arraigned and with his court-appointed attorney he entered a plea of Not Guilty. On March 2, 1964, he was ordered examined by a team of psychiatrists. Upon receipt of their reports the subject was determined legally sane and trial was set for May 11, 1964. On April 29, 1964, the subject was allowed to change his plea to Guilty as Charged, and sentencing was withheld pending receipt of a Presentence Investigation." (This is a case history of the criminal to help the judge determine the sentence.)

Newspaper account of the sentencing: "The murderer, age twenty-nine, listened impassively as the judge imposed sentence and told him, 'You will never walk the street again. I've given a great deal of thought to this vile crime the past two and a half weeks,' the judge said. 'I've never felt an eye for an eye and a tooth for a tooth is true justice. The court's awesome task is to administer a just sentence and deter others from committing crimes. I am the father of four children, I realize how the parents of this little girl have suffered. The testimony from four psychiatrists was appalling. Somewhere in your youth and environment you had something wrong with you. You are not motivated by the usual emotions. There are psychiatrists at the state penitentiary. If I send you to prison for life you will never walk the streets again. The other case of the killing of the nineteen-year-old girl will be held over your head and you will never be considered for parole. My only hope is that the time in prison you spend with your conscience leads to an understanding of your deed. God is the only one to forgive you. I sentence you to confinement in state prison at hard labor for life, and may God be with you."

A prison psychiatrist, 1971: did an evaluation for the parole and probation commission: "This inmate has never received a D.R. (disciplinary report). I do believe that he is a good candidate to be sent to one of the new centers in the city. As an inmate employee there. This way we can see how he will function in an environment like those centers. He has seen the parole commission for two consecutive years, but so far no definite plans have been made. As we know he has been an excellent inmate according to his record. This does not let us predict his behavior. But on the other hand if we do not expose him to a different environment we will not know how he acts. I will recommend that he be sent to another institution to be exposed to a different type of environment and be observed for future parole consideration."

A prison psychiatrist, 1976: "In summary, this psychiatric evaluation agrees with previous ones as well as with the psychological testing, that this man's moral conscience, his disregard for social demands and problems, his needs to wrestle with the basic issues which resulted in his deviant behavior, show that it has been virtually impossible for him to make the necessary in-depth changes, and in consequence, he is not ready for major responsibilities. His partial success in functioning during incarceration is understandable because he works better in a structured environment. It is doubtful that neither psychotherapy nor pharmacotherapeutic measures could bring a major change to his personality makeup at present."

A Team Evaluation (of prison officials) 1978: "His prison adjustment has continued to be excellent throughout. Nevertheless, he is able to affect whatever behavior mechanisms that are necessary to bring about his desired ends. Apparently at this he is attempting to present a facade of mild-mannered well-adjustment. He expressed to the team members that his only avenue out at this time was through psychological evaluations that he had received on his own behalf. The team accepts these attempts at good adjustment. Nevertheless, the team could not overlook earlier evaluations that indicate that he is beyond empathy or remorse. Therefore, the team cannot at this time in good conscience make a recommendation that would bring about this man's early release. *He is viewed by the team as being extremely dangerous, totally without feeling, and an extreme menace to society."*

Now let us recall the words of the judge who sentenced this multiple murderer: "If I send you to prison for life you will never walk the streets again. The other case of the killing of the nineteen-year-old, which you have confessed, will be held over your head and you will never be considered for parole."

How naive can a judge be? A life sentence has never meant until the criminal dies. In this particular state a life sentence means only seven years before the criminal is considered for parole. The parole board actually has the power to parole a criminal the day he is received in prison! Most states have similar rules.

In this murderer's case, some psychologists in a sex-offender program are trying to get this murderer sent to their open-type (living as free men) program—a program where I know for a fact one of their sex-offenders has murdered a woman on the premises. Luckily for society, a prison psychiatrist has blocked this murderer's transfer.

How long will the state keep this man in prison? That's anybody's guess!

STEVE

"Crime is like a habit," the rapist said. "As you get more involved in it you become more addicted to it, and should I say, it's like habitual? You just keep on and you get influenced by it, and you see that you are able to get on better by not working. So you go on and take something from somebody else.

"As I got more involved into shoplifting and from that to higher things—B&E (Breaking and Entering) and robbery. It was a sort of a thrill. Sometimes it was really exciting. It was fun, really, to be sneaking around in people's houses when they were in there and not knowing you're around and all. You're creeping things off.

"You start out with little things. Shoplifting candy, cookies, or ice cream. Nothing really big. But if you get caught you go to the detention center, and you sit around in there until you're scheduled to go to court—juvenile court. And you go to court and they tell your parents why don't you try to keep your kid in line. And you go back home, and you start doing the same thing over again. Stealing bicycles was just part of growing up.

"It's like a stage you go through. You start lower and go up higher. From something simple to something more complex. You just go through stages. I wouldn't work. I always went in somebody's house and stole something. Then I went in for strong-arm robbery—purse snatching."

Question: "How did you pick out the houses you were going to burglarize?"

Answer: "Just by walking around till you find one that looks like you can get in. Usually in the daytime the windows would be up, so it was very easy. We broke in while people were working. At night we could spot where the people were in the house, and if they're watching TV we can count on them being into the program, so we creep on in and take something that won't be noticed right away.

"Mostly we went in at night, and mostly we went in on women living alone. I had my getaway all situated, I knew how I was going to go in and I knew how I was going to come out. The way I was going to come out I always had open, so I could rush on out if I had to. I wasn't scared of getting shot—usually they're scareder of you than you are of them. By them waking up and seeing you, they're more frightened than you are. It was exciting. It was fun.

"If I get into the house when you're asleep, usually I can ease in and get what I want and ease out, and you won't know about it until morning. But I had a knife sometimes, not for protection, but it was used for clicking doors or cutting screens, of just punching a hole in the screen and open up the hook and open the door or window.

"I wore dark clothes and sneakers. I used to do this all the time. I got to the point where if I got caught I could scare the person off to put fear in them till I could get away.

"When you're B&E-ing you usually don't have to worry about anybody if you wait until late at night when everybody's asleep. I could run real good, that was my getaway, plus I can duck and dodge. I know the section pretty good, and the cop cars can't go where I can go—through alleys and up over fences, they got to go all around. While they're going around I'm coming out. I would always hide, anywhere I feel you won't look.

"If you want to snatch a pocket book, you just hide until they come by and then you sneak on up behind them and snatch and run.

"I did a lot of B&Es, and I did strong armed robbery, but I never robbed with a gun, or robbed a store, just purse snatching.

"I'll be walking down the street and I'll start feeling an urge, or a sensation or some kind of feeling, that's saying, 'Man, you ought to do something tonight, go ahead. Go ahead and do something.' And then I start concentrating on that. I start thinking about it. Then I just want to go ahead and do it. It was getting about every night. I like burglarizing better than work. I was making a lot more, sometimes on one or two jobs, than I could working all the time. I knew it (burglarizing) was a better thing, where I could go get money. As soon as the money got low that's when I'd go back. If it took me seven nights straight to get what I wanted, I'd do it, but that's the only reason I'd do it all the time.

"One time when I got busted the police were reading the pattern. When you do something it gets reported, and it will get reported from this point over here, and then one will be reported from over there. Then they'll report one from over here, and they'll try to figure out where you're gonna be, so they'll patrol over here. Cause they figure this is where you're coming from tonight. They're gonna lay over here for you. And if you do come over there you'll get busted."

Question: "At first you were just doing B&Es for the money. Now when did you start having sex with them?"

Answer: "It's sort of like a stage you go into. I'm not weird, you know. But like I said, it's really like a pattern you go through.

"When you go in, you gotta make it known that you're in there for business and not pleasure or playing. We got to the point where we'd look a place all over, and maybe there wasn't nothing in there that we wanted to take out. And if we knew there was money in there but we couldn't find out where it was, we'd have to wake her. So we would go to her bedroom and grabbed her somewhere around the neck, so she know we mean business. And you kind of put a little pressure on her neck. When you squeezing her neck she can't talk. So you say if you act right we let up on you. This way she wakes up with your hand on her neck. And you're rough with her too. Ain't no telling what might be going through her head, waking up and finding herself in that predicament. So she don't know what's happening to her. Me not having a gun or knife or anything, I had to grab them. Cutting the wind off keeps them from screaming. Putting a little pressure, and at the same time telling them what you want to know, and getting them under control, so that they'll be in your control and whatever you want them to do they'll do it, cause they know that you have the force and the power to take them out of the picture if necessary."

Question: "Did you ever have anyone pass out on you?"

Answer: "No, because you don't apply full pressure so that you kill them. You just only want what you said understood, so that they'll act right and do anything you want them to do.

"Young women are more fun, but older women have more money and jewelry. There was this one old lady that told us she had cancer, so we didn't have sex with her."

Question: "Tell me about the last young lady you broke in on."

Answer: "At this particular point money wasn't on my mind. I guess this girl had really turned me on. And then what really helped it out, we couldn't just get into this house normally like going through the window. We had to figure out a different way, like going to the doorbell hoping she's going to open the door, and ask her where a street was. So this is what we made up to do. We planning to say something that will distract her attention, like ask her where this street is cause we new in town. Something to distract her attention and put an impression that we're on the good side, but to get her to commit herself so that we'll have a way in.

"So after we had made up to do that, we rang the doorbell, and I was hoping that she'd come cause I really wanted in on this one. I really had got built up. I knew, after seeing this fine girl walking, I wasn't going in for the money. She was foxy too. And white. It really turned me on. So when she came to the door she did just what I was hoping she'd do. I said to myself, if she comes to the door and opens the door I'm gonna step in between her and the door. She came to the door, calling, 'Alright, here I come, here I come.' I guess she was expecting someone, and she was. She had a date, and she must have thought we were the date.

"When she came to the door and I stepped between her and the door, I couldn't even think what I was going to say—my made up story. So I said, excuse me, can you tell me where—and I couldn't think of a street. And right then I knew it was all over, playing games, it was back to business. But we had got our way in, and that was our way in. So I had to grab her then, and when I did she stumbled back and fell and I fell on top of her. I grabbed her around the throat so she couldn't scream. And that was all it took."

Question: "Did she report the rape."

Answer: "She must have. She probably wouldn't have if she wouldn't have been caught in that situation like that. Quite naturally by her not being ready or whatever she had to bring up her reasons to why she wasn't ready. She probably was frightened some, quite naturally. That would frighten someone, but after I left it was like she told me goodbye, she said, 'Bye, I'll see you later.' And during the period when we was having sex it was just like a normal relation, you know, she was having a good time. She was having a good time."

Question: "What if you hadn't been caught when you were. Would you have continued to break in and rape women?"

Answer: "Most likely this (raping) would have become a way of life. It would have developed into that. Every chance I'd got I would be doing it. Because all the time that I was coming up and going through the stages, then this would just be another stage. I would have started doing that so much that it would have been my way of having sex. I probably would have just stopped having dates with girls or going out. I'd of probably have went looking for sex this way. Because that would have been exciting. Because it would have been some kind of sensation in it. Yeah, most likely it would have developed into that. I'd have got excitement out of it and that would be my way of having sex.

"If I'd kept on and kept on I would have just developed into taking sex, making them have sex against their will. That would have been just outright taking it, like I took money. You just done develop this take and it's been a fixed part of you now for so many months or years or whatever, and you are forming a habit. And as many times as you do it, you become more accustomed to it, and you keep on and you get more accustomed to it. And now it's becoming a habit. And you do this every time you go out and find a lady by herself. You do it out of habit because you did it the last time, you'll do it this time. And it's a continuation of the first time. And it keeps on. And it becomes habitual."

ANDREW

This rapist was arrested for Breaking and Entering with Intent to Commit Rape only *seven hours* after he had been paroled from the state sex offender program, where he had spent three and a half years in therapy. He was discharged as "cured of his sexual proclivities." Someone forgot to tell his latest rape victim that he was "cured"!

This rapist has *five felony convictions*—why has he not been convicted as a habitual felon? It takes only three convictions to be convicted as an habitual felon, and with this conviction the criminal is sent to prison for life *with no chance for parole.*

A felony is any crime that carries as punishment a *prison* sentence. A misdemeanor is any crime that does not carry a prison sentence—usually a crime whose penalty is less than one year. Misdemeanor sentences may carry a penalty of *jail* time, but *not prison* time.

This *"five time loser"* is now sentenced to prison for "life less 118 days of county jail time." Isn't that asinine, to credit a criminal with the time he has already served in the county jail awaiting trial, if a life sentence *means* a life sentence? But a life sentence in many states only means that the criminal must serve a few years (in the state where this rapist is incarcerated a life sentence means only seven years). So that county jail time of 118 days means that this rapist can be considered for another parole after only six years and seven months.

This rapist "graduated" from reform school when he became twenty-one years old. He immediately committed another felony, was arrested and sent to prison. After each stint in prison, he returned to his old habits. At the time this rapist was discharged from the sex offender program, he had reached the ripe old age of twenty-six. More than ten years of his life had been spent in reform schools and prisons. And in reform school and prison, this rapist perfected his skill in picking locks.

This criminal followed a predictable pattern as he graduated to crimes of a more serious nature. When he first started stealing as a boy, he took bicycles and balls from yards. Then he started going up on people's porches to steal. And when he saw no one was bothering him he became braver and started trying to get into houses.

The criminal says, "When I started breaking into houses I climbed through windows. It was real fun, because at the time I was just breaking into the house to get petty change. If I found ten dollars or something like that I thought I was rich. At the time I was really having fun. Then my two brothers started doing it with me.

"We'd go in a house and have all kinds of fun, like maybe take eggs out of the refrigerator and throw at each other and all over the walls. We'd go in the bedrooms and throw stuff out of the drawers. We'd just be plundering. Sometimes we just tore the whole house while the people were gone. While I'm in a house I feel kind of like in a toyland. Kind of excitement. Kind of makes you feel like that you're in control of the situation.

"As I started getting bigger and bigger I just started wanting more money out of the house. So I was having to break into a lot of houses. I know there's probably something wrong with me, but with burglary, I really have fun. Why should I work all day, when I can do something exciting like burglary? After I got where I could really pick locks, if I stayed out all night I could hit about twenty places. I mostly burglarized houses.

"I only woke people up when I was burglarizing their house if I wanted something I knew they had. Like his wife having a big diamond ring. I'd wake them up by shining a light in their eyes. Usually I would wake up the man and tell him I didn't want any trouble or anybody to get hurt. I wanted him to wake up his wife so that way she wouldn't scream and holler. I only woke them up if I had a weapon, a pistol. And then I would tell them what I wanted. I always had some kind of mask on. Sometimes I would get a tape recorder and have my partner talk into it, so they wouldn't recognize my voice. Then after I woke them up I'd just turn on the tape recorder.

"What I usually steal is if they got real nice silverware. I'll usually look in the buffet and drawers to see if they got any coin collection or stamp collection, something like that. Then I'll go upstairs and go in the bedroom and take all the jewelry while they're sleeping. Most of the time I leave the back door cracked open for an escape. And I always parked my car within running distance."

This criminal would rather burglarize two story houses, because he figures all the people sleep upstairs and he can go around downstairs without worrying too much about noise. The criminal says, "I got so brave at the time I was doing burglaries that I wouldn't really care whether the people were in there or not, in the nighttime."

"Now in the daytime," this criminal says, "I had it figured out how I could get the people out of the house. I'll ride around until I pick out a house I like, then I'll watch it a couple of days. Then I'll watch when the man leaves the house and I'll follow him and see where he works. Lot of the people have their name on the mailbox, and if they don't I'll just hang around until the mailman comes, then I'll go look at their mail to see what their name is. Then I'll go look it up in the telephone book, and that gives me a telephone number. I knew the man wasn't ever there during the day, so I just phoned his wife and told her that he had been in an accident, and that he was up in the hospital, and could she come as quickly as possible. So while she's going to the hospital, I go in the house and get anything I want."

The criminal continues, "Most of the young and middle-aged couples are both working, so I don't have to worry about anybody being home during the day. If they have a maid, and I can't get rid of the maid and the wife too, then I just wait and go in at nighttime. I always have a flashlight. If you have a bright flashlight it will startle them and they can't look into your face. And I like to use a ski mask too. I always had seven or eight of them. I always cut phone wires too, before I go in the house."

As a burglar the criminal makes this statement, "I wasn't breaking into too many houses. Like I might not even need the money or anything that I'm going to get out of the stuff, but I just break into houses to break into them. I always carry burglar tools in my car when I'm out to burglarize a place. And when I think that I can't get in the house any other way but with burglar tools, I'll carry them up to the house. I've got about a whole locksmith's kit. And I know how to use just about any kind of tool a locksmith handles.

"It got so that anytime a burglary happened the police would question me. So I decided to go to another state. But before I left, I closed out my bank account, then went around writing as many checks as I could to get money and new clothes. And I knew when I got to the other state I was going to go back into burglarizing."

Question: "You were never convicted for rape in your home state. When did you change over from burglarizing to have sex with the women in the houses you burglarized?"

Answer: "I have broke into houses with a lot of different people, and some of the people that I had broken into with wanted to go ahead and rape the woman. At that time I hadn't gotten into that, so I just told them, 'No, we're not going to have nothing of that.' So pretty soon when I started breaking into them by myself I'd see the woman laying up there by herself and I'd start getting that idea. And I think that is mainly where the idea came into my head."

Question: "Tell me about the first woman you did?"

Answer: "You mean, the first woman I raped?" (Uh-huh). "It was during a burglary and really I didn't have no resistance at all. All she was afraid of was I going to hurt her. And that was about it. I don't really think I enjoyed it. Because really, I think, like a lot of the rapists I have talked to in the sex offender program have told me, that they expect the victim to fight back. And when the victims don't fight back it just—like a lot of sex offenders told me that they would just quit if the victim didn't fight back. Or either they would hit them, knock them up aside the head or something like that to get them to fight back. And if they still didn't get a fight back they would just quit.

"Now a lot of people it doesn't work for like that. You just have to judge the people. A lot of people if you do fight them back they're gonna run. And a lot of people if they don't fight back it turns them off and they can't go through with the rape. So I think mainly you got to judge. The victim has probably a hard task judging them because they're frightened and all like that and I think they have a hard time making that instant judgment. And then again they could make a wrong judgment and it could be fatal to them."

Less than two months after he was released from his second prison term, and still on parole, he committed his first (admitted) rape: "The first girl I raped I never picked her out. I just broke into the house and there she was. And she was the only one in the house. She must have been about twenty-two. She was asleep when I went in, and I was wearing crepe soled shoes and she didn't hear me.

"I shined the flashlight in her face. First of all I told her this was a robbery. That I wanted all of her jewelry and stuff like that. So I wasn't worrying about her seeing me 'cause it was dark in the room and stuff like that, and the light was in her face. I was wearing a mask at the time. She told me that she didn't have any jewelry. Well, it was just a game anyway, because I had already ramshackled the whole house without waking her up. And I had got all the jewelry and everything out of her room, too. So after she told me she didn't have any jewelry, I told her, 'You don't?' Anyway I just got on with her, and she asked me, what was I doing, and I said, 'Look, I'm going to rape you.' And she started crying a little bit, and told me not to. And at that time I started to leave. But for some reason I started talking to her and she just finally quit crying. And then I just started fondling her, and pretty soon I had her down on the bed and was raping her."

The rapist says, "At one time I thought that she was enjoying it. That's mainly why I went on through with it, because if she'd have put up some kind of fight with me I wouldn't of never went on through with it. Like I'm the type if they'd put up some kind of fight there wasn't no way I was going to go on through with it."

Question: "How did this rape end?"

Answer: "I just got out of bed. And she had a bathrobe over there, and I went into the closet and got another bathrobe. And I just turned her over and tied her hands behind her back with one bathrobe, and tied her to the bed with the other one. And I always carried some tape along with me. I put tape over her mouth and that was it. She just lay there like a zombie. And so I just walked out and picked up the loot by the door and went on my way.

"There was this girl I went in on especially to rape. I saw her lying on the bed asleep, so I went in to her apartment real easy. And I took off my shoes and socks and eased on the bed before she woke up. And she started screaming, and struggling. And for some reason I had a feeling this one was going to give me trouble, so I took a hunting knife with me. And when she started screaming I put my hand over her mouth and showed her the knife and told her I was going to hurt her if she screamed. And she shook her head that she wouldn't. So I was about to put down the knife and she started struggling and I dropped the knife and she got it and started screaming. I got scared and grabbed my shoes and ran out the front door.

"I think every time I have broken into a house I have broke in there with the intention of ra—for another reason, mainly to burglarize and steal and stuff like that. I think the only difference was, when I got busted here in this state the first time, for Breaking and Entering with Intent to Commit Rape, at that time I knew the girl. I got mad at the girl so at the time I broke into her house with the intention of beating her up. So when I got in there I decided that instead of beating her up it would be more harmful to her if I raped her. So at the time she was in bed asleep. So I woke her up. So I woke her up. And she asked me what I wanted and I told her I was going to rape her. And then she started screaming and crying, so I put my hand over her mouth and told her not to scream and cry or I was going to have to beat her up. I told her I didn't want to hurt her, so she started to cry. And I'm just the type person I'm weak for a woman who cries, it just gets to me. And I just told her, 'Look, if you'll stop crying I'll leave.' And I said, 'Are you going to stop crying?', and she shook her head

'Yes.' So I said, 'O.K. I'm going to leave.' And this girl knew where I was staying at, and by the time I left she went ahead and called the police on me. When I left her I went on back to where I was staying at, and pretty soon the police came and that's when I was arrested."

Question: "Did you think she wouldn't turn you in?"

Answer: "I don't know. At the time that I went back to my apartment my feelings was all, I just couldn't think straight in other words. And I just didn't know whether she would turn me in or not. I think that's what I was thinking. I just didn't know whether she would turn me in or not. And I think that's why I stayed in my own apartment."

The rapist continues: "A lot of victims don't want to go through that hassle of going through the courts and I thought she was going to drop the charges, especially because not too much happened. I understood from people up in the jail that she had already been in the state hospital (mental hospital) before."

Question: "What does that have to do with anything?"

Answer: "I'm not sure. My lawyer told me that he had heard that about her and he was checking into it. But he told me that if it's true that she could get up on the stand and if he can get enough on her past record that he will just destroy her on the stand.

"At the time I had been charged with this other one, and the lawyer said, don't worry about that either, because I can probably get a lot of information on her, too."

Question: "But that victim was a stranger to you?"

Answer: "Yeap. So the lawyer said we can either try to beat it, which I think we probably have a very good chance of doing it, because first of all they might not get up on the stand and testify. And if they do we can try to destroy their credibility. And I think we probably have a pretty good chance of beating them. Or you can go talk to these two psychiatrists and see what they want to do. I asked him what did he think I should do, and he said that he thought I should go talk to the two psychiatrists."

On the recommendation of the psychiatric reports (which stated that the rapist was a sociopath) this rapist was committed to the state program for mentally disordered sex offenders, where he was "treated" for three and a half years. The very day he was discharged from this program, he committed another burglary with attempted rape, for which he was arrested, tried, and sent to prison for life.

Question: "Do you think that you'll stop raping?"

Answer: "Really *I don't know if I'll stop* until I have a long enough time out on the streets to see if I will—to see if I do have enough will power to control myself. I think that's the whole thing. *I don't think you're ever cured.*

I think it's if you have enough will power not to do it. If you have enough feelings for the woman not to do it."

Question: "You never had any feelings for the woman to begin with, did you?"

Answer: "No, I was just looking at them like I said, as objects. I know one guy that went in to rape this lady, and she started to talk to him and asked him why he was doing this and all. And they got to talking about it and he didn't rape her. But she set up an appointment for him to come back the next day to talk some more and when he did she had the police waiting for him.

"I know I'm not going to stop raping on my own. I'm gonna need a lot of help when I get out to stop. If I don't have nobody to make me stop I'm going right back to raping and B&Es. In fifteen minutes work I can get a thousand dollars easy by B&Es.

"I can remember when I got out of the penitentiary and the boys' reform school, like I always stay straight a couple of months. I don't want to go back in. And then I start thinking about I don't think the police are gonna catch me anyways. And I'll go back breaking and raping again. But usually when I'm out there most of the contact I have is with burglars and stuff like that. I really don't mind working when it's something I enjoy. When I'm around other people and they're not working, out there enjoying theirselves all day and I guess they plant the idea into my head—'Ah, you better come on in. Let's go break into this house. We can get as much money in fifteen minutes as what you make at your job in a week.' And I go to thinking about that and pretty soon I go to breaking into houses again. So I think it's just mainly how I'll feel when I get out. *At least in seven years I'll be up for parole.*"

DANIEL

This rapist has an F.B.I. record that dates from the age of fifteen and starts out with an arrest for prowling. I interviewed him when he was thirty-eight and had amassed many arrests for Prowling, Breaking and Entering with Intent to Commit a Felony, Rape. For only one of his past offenses had he served any time in prison—a ten year sentence for which he was paroled in three and a half years. The rapist speaks very bitterly of this sentence and his commitment to reform school:

"I got to thinking, here I was. I got arrested once, twice and never even got nothing, except for a year or an indefinite period. And reform school. I got ten years in prison for *intent* to commit a felony—B&E with intent to commit a felony. *That burned the hell out of me.* It'd be alright if I go to jail for committing murder. It has to be worthwhile, you know. Something really has to happen, to have to kill them or even shoot them."

Let's look at the official reports on this *attempted felony* which were written by a parole officer *after* the rapist pleaded guilty to the offense, to assist the judge in making a decision in the sentencing of the prisoner. The 1964 report reads:

"Police Report: Received a call to go to this address to confirm an attempted rape. As the cruiser neared the house they were halted by cries of help from next door. At that time a female told them she was afraid because someone had just tried to rape her neighbor. The police advised her to remain calm, and they proceeded to the original destination next door, where upon arrival they observed blood splattered on the wooden doorstep. The victim met them at the door and gave them entry to the house. The house is a single bedroom frame home, and it was noted that a path of fresh blood was evident from the porch into the bedroom. And the complainant was bleeding from the facial and mouth areas. The bedding on the bed was disarranged and the victim was very obviously upset and injured. She was dressed in slacks and a shirt, an outfit suited for street wear.

"The victim claims she went into her bedroom and laid down on the bed. Shortly thereafter she opened her eyes and saw a white male standing over her. He told her to remain silent, but the victim screamed and the subject began striking her repeatedly in the area of the face. At this time the next door neighbor screamed, 'Betty, are you alright?' The defendant then, apparently frightened, went through the living room, through the kitchen and exited the house through the back door. He leaped off the porch and started running through the alley. The victim then ran next door and remained with her neighbor until shortly before the officers arrived on the scene.

"The victim gave the police a very good description of the assailant, as did a former roommate of the victim, she stated that at approximately 0100 hours she had been seated on her porch and had observed a white male with a dark shirt and light pants in an alley located behind the residence of the victim. The next door neighbor stated that shortly before 0200 hours she had been awakened by screams and had screamed back, 'Betty, what is the matter?' She then observed a white male exit by the back exit, leap from the porch, and begin running up the alley. The neighbor's bedroom window is about twenty-five feet from the victim's bedroom window.

"After talking to the police the victim remembered that during the entire period the defendant was attacking her he had the zipper to his pants down. The victim could see his white undershorts."

"Defendant's Statement: The defendant admits the offense, and states that he was over at a bar, had a couple of drinks, then went back to the boat where he worked and started the freezer. Then he got into his car and rode around, parked his car, and walked toward the victim's house. The defendant said he saw a car go by and stop at the victim's house. The car was driven by a girl,

and another girl came out of the house to talk with her. The girls stood by the car for a long time, with the defendant standing in a dark portion of the street, listening to their conversation. The defendant stated that after one of the girls drove off the other went into the house. He went close to the house and waited awhile before going into the house. The defendant states the girls were talking about their boyfriends while he was standing in the shadows.

"The defendant admits going through the back door, going into the house, at which time he stood at the victim's door until she looked up and screamed. The defendant states that he jumped on her very quickly and put his hand on her mouth until she promised to quit screaming. However, when he released his hand she screamed again, and this time the defendant indicated that he struck her with his fist and left. The defendant stated that he left through the back door and ran through the alley. The defendant offered an explanation for his pants being open, by saying that he had a bad rash and therefore did not wear undershorts, and during the struggle his pants came open. The defendant stated that he had on a pair of tight continental pants and they came open during the struggle and that he zipped them up as he left the scene. The defendant states that he did not break into the house to rape the victim, and that on probation he is sure he can make a good adjustment."

"*Defendant's attitude:* The defendant did not appear to be too concerned at the time of the interview, and gave the impression that someone had made a bad mistake in his case. The defendant's attitude has changed considerably since being committed to the county jail, in that he gave the police department a handwritten statement witnessed by three detectives indicating, 'That I was going to see if I could get a piece of ass if it was possible. The reason that I hit the girl was that when she started to scream I got scared and hit this girl. After I hit her she just kept on and so I took off through the back door. I had a towel so I wouldn't leave my fingerprints while I was in the house.'

"The assailant had an automatic pistol in his auto when arrested and the detective who arrested him believes the assailant had the pistol on his person when he committed the B&E.

"The victim has moved to a different residence."

Nine years after the crime just described, this criminal committed rape that resulted in his being sent to the state mental hospital as a Mentally Disordered Sex Offender to be "treated" for his aberrant sex habits. Following three and a half years of incarceration in the sex offender program, this rapist was sentenced to Life in prison. At the time of the interview with this rapist, he was eligible for parole!

Let us consider the present offense for which the rapist is in prison. The official report is a Presentence Investigation, brought up to date. The Police Report: "Two girls came home around 12:30 A.M. and were inside their house at which time an unknown white male with a sheet over his head, jumped out and pushed a shotgun in one victim's stomach. The suspect pointed the shotgun at her and told her to lay face down across the bed, and he also told the other white female to lay face down across the bed and began to have sexual intercourse with her. During the incident the suspect had the shotgun under his right arm. The suspect then told the women to lay flat for ten minutes and he fled the scene. First victim then ran to her boyfriend's house and called the police. It was determined that among the articles missing were approximately twenty pairs of women's bikini panties, five bras, five slips, seven bathing suits and cash—approximately $60.00.

"Eventually a white male was arrested for rape and he matched the description of the person involved in this offense. A search warrant was issued for the subject's residence, and the property taken in this offense (panties, et al.) was found in residence of the subject.

"The first victim viewed a line-up and identified the rapist by voice identification as the person who had raped the other victim in her presence.

"The prior arrest record of this subject indicates that the rapist was sentenced in 1964 to ten years in prison for the offense of attempted rape. The circumstances are similar to the subject's present rape offense."

"*Detective's report:* In addition to the rape case he was arrested on, and the two victims of the offense just related, the rapist has raped two juveniles and *has recorded the rape on tape of the juveniles crying during the rape.*"

The report continues: "The rapist's M.O. is that he would rape the women, then steal their underclothing. This subject also raped his next door neighbor. She did not report the rape until approximately four months later, at the time of the investigation of the present crime."

The following is the rapist's description of one of his rapes: "I met this girl on the beach. She was a runaway, but I didn't find that out until later on. I asked her if she wanted to go for a ride, and she said yes, so I took her for a ride. Took her back to the beach, and as I dropped her off she said she was waiting for somebody to come and pick her up and she couldn't get ahold of him. And I said, 'I'll take you home.' And then she started wising off to me a little bit and it made me mad. So I just took her on to my place and got in there and well, things happened and I just sort of raped her a little bit.

"I only had to strike her one time to get her to stop struggling. And when it was over I took her right back to where I picked her up at. And she made a phone call, and I don't know whether she was playing games or not. And she told me that somebody was on the way. And I said, 'Are you sure? I'll take you home, or wherever she wanted to go.' She said she was alright, so I turned around and took off."

The rapist speaks about women in general: "There's good girls and there's bad girls. Psychologically I got messed up with a bunch of females. And a lot of them, 'Hey, how about going somewhere?' If I had the money they had the time. If I didn't have the money they didn't have the time. A few of them refused to go out with me and I knew them for a long time.

"I raped when I was feeling depressed. How many times women used me. Here I am trying to be Mr. Good Guy and bam. You spend money, you try to get attention. And if you're an attention getter like that you can have all kinds of people. So I just got where I'd buy just one or two drinks and quit. I try to do more talking than drinking. The more drinks I bought, the madder I got. Here I am sitting in a bar alone and rejected, and that's (rape) the only way I could fight back. *I never intended to hurt nobody, but the law don't see it that way.*

"Committing crimes showed that I had a heart. I didn't shoot nobody and I didn't cut nobody."

MARK

Mark had an engaging personality. His red hair was cut attractively, he was neatly dressed, always polite, and he smiled often.

It hadn't taken long hours, or even minutes to get Mark to talk freely, for he was quite eager to be in the spotlight again. In the hospital, where he had spent three and a half years in a treatment program for sex offenders, he had been given an enormous amount of personal attention and freedom. Although he continually failed to benefit from the vocational rehabilitation programs, the hospital staff kept changing him from program to program to keep his "motivational level high." In prison he missed this special treatment. In prison he was treated like all the other inmates, and like the other inmates he either obeyed the rules or received disciplinary reports.

One month after his twenty-fifth birthday Mark was arrested for rape. When I talked to Mark he was twenty-six years of age and serving a life sentence in the state prison.

Listen to Mark's description of how he feels when he is planning and committing his rapes:

"The thing that turned me on the most was the excitement of getting away with it. Violence had a lot to do with it, but the main thing was the excitement and getting away with it. I thought a lot about getting caught, simply because of where I was at, and the situation I was in. It would have been so easy to catch me. And doing it right there is a lot more exciting, as all the cars are going by and I'm snickering, 'Look what I'm getting away with, you fools!' I must have parked out there forty or fifty times.

"When I hit her I enjoyed it. That really set me off. I could commit as much violence as I wanted to. The excitement of doing it and getting away with it. I was picturing cars and helicopters, but I was where they weren't. I liked hurting them—I enjoyed it.

"The whole time I was at work I would think about it. Then when I got off work I would ride around, or go home, until after dark. Sometimes when I was watching TV I'd tell my wife I was going out for a pack of cigarettes— and wouldn't come home for two weeks.

This rapist always committed his rapes on the shoulder of a heavily traveled interstate highway. His Modus Operandi never varied. His only victims were hitchhikers. "Nothing in particular about a girl turns me on. All the girls hitchhiking were young hippy-type girls. So far as being choosy, or going to a supermarket and picking them out, I never had to." He also knew where to find them. "You could always go to the beaches and find girls hitchhiking there, even at three or four in the morning. I had a regular route I used to take. I would ride from the lower end to the upper end and back— about twenty-five miles of beaches. I used to be at the beaches every night, in the same car every time, and see the same cops every night, and they never stopped me. Those cops should have known that a man alone like that has to be up to something."

There are hundreds of cars along the beaches every night. Mark would always pick up his victims in a spot where it was dark. Some of the girls he passed by simply because it would be a bad time to pick them up—too much light or a heavily populated area, although cars near by were never a bother. Then too, it was how he felt—how big a chance he wanted to take. The victims were always available.

After Mark had chosen his victim he would reach over and open the front door for her, but he made sure the inside car light would not come on. As she got into the seat beside him he would take her under control by encircling her neck with his arm and pulling her down on the seat saying, "Don't move and I won't hurt you. Lay still." Most of the time the women did just as he said. If they struggled he would threaten them—"I don't want to hurt you, just lay still"— and said "Some I'd have to hit, or slap, or something like that." He carried a sharp weapon that he often held to their necks.

Mark would drive with his victim onto an interstate highway, across some bridges, and as far away as thirty-five miles from the point of abduction. "I have often wondered why I drove so far, and I guess it was the added thrill of the possibility of being stopped for a traffic violation and getting away with it."

When he had cleared the city congestion and found a spot where bushes were growing beside the interstate, he would pull his car onto the shoulder of the highway next to the bushes. He would then force his victim from the car into the bushes where he would rape her. It all depended on how he felt that night whether he would beat her, or leave her out on the highway. If he felt "really nasty" he would leave her on the highway without clothes.

"I know the girls were scared to death. Sometimes on the way back they would sit up with me, right by me. After the sex was over it was like we knew each other—*not all the time*. But most of the time. The fear they had in their hearts, the fear was gone. O.K., the fear probably never left them until I got in the car and we headed back to town. But once we started down the road it was gone."

Jane became a victim of Mark's only two days after he had assaulted another girl. She was hitchhiking one evening about 10:00 P.M. when Mark gave her a lift. With Jane, Mark was very friendly—at first. He told her his name was "Roy," and during their conversation "Roy" mentioned three times that he wanted to "boogie." Jane kept denying him, thinking that the word "boogie" meant to have sexual intercourse.

Furious at her denials, Mark grabbed Jane around the neck and placed a sharp object to her throat. The sharp object was later found to be that ever-present paint scraper. Mark pulled Jane down on the seat with him and began riding around the south side of the city.

At one point Jane tried to escape. However, Mark grabbed her and hit her in the mouth. He also cut her on the wrist with the paint scraper. After this Jane lay still on the seat. Mark told her to take off her bra, which she did, and he began fondling her breasts underneath her blouse. Then he unbuckled her pants and began fondling her vaginal area.

While Mark's attention was divided between his driving and his molesting her, Jane found a good chance to escape. Even though the car was moving, she jumped out, skinning herself on the pavement, and ran to a taxicab for help. The taxi took Jane to the hospital, where police were called. Jane could describe Mark, but like his other victims, she could give very little information about his car.

It took bits and pieces of memory from all of Mark's victims (who had reported the rapes) for the police to identify the car. The police then staked out the car in front of Mark's mother's house. When Mark came out and got into the car the detectives arrested him. He wasn't very brave then. He didn't try to fight or run or do anything. He just went along with them, acting very cocky, as if he was a big man. The police found the sharpened paint scraper when they impounded his car and secured a warrant to search for it.

The detectives compiled a photo-pack to show to the victims. A photo-pack consists usually of ten photographs of people that look like the suspect and whose descriptions fit those given by the victims. All of the victims, immediately identified the photo of Mark as the man who had committed offenses against them.

When the detectives interrogated Mark, he readily admitted to all of the offenses with which he had been charged. He was a suspect in many other rapes, for which he was not charged. He was also suspect in the murder of a girl whose body was found in the area.

When Mark was arrested on November 25, ten days after his attack upon Jane and only twelve days after his brutal assault upon another victim, he was placed in the county jail without bond. This meant that he could not post bail and be allowed to remain free until his trial. Many, many rapists are allowed to post bail and remain free to continue their sexual assaults, and to threaten their previous victims, until, and if, they are brought to trial.

In Court, with the approval of his attorney, Mark entered a plea of guilty as charged. There were six counts (charges) against him: Rape, Aggravated Assault, Kidnapping, Imprisonment, Assault with Intent to Commit Rape, and Battery. At the time of pleading guilty, sentencing was deferred, as usual, until a presentence investigation could be made.

A presentence investigation (P.S.I.) is a case study of the defendant's life. It is a fact-finding study conducted by a probation-parole officer after a jury has found a defendant guilty, or after the defendant had pleaded guilty. It helps the judge determine what type of sentence would be best to impose on the defendant.

In the presentence investigation the officer notes both the good as well as the bad in the defendant's background. Included in the P.S.I. are the following: the official police reports on the circumstances of the crime; the defendant's version of the crime; the victim's version of the crime; the offender's verified criminal record; the community reaction to the crime; the reaction of the offender's family and friends; and the appraisal of the crime on the part of the police and the victim. Also included are any psychiatric evaluations made on the offender. These items by no means cover the complete contents of the presentence investigation.

Mark had an interesting presentence investigation. He had raped perhaps fifty girls, yet in the statements Mark gave the two psychiatrists who examined him, he said "he had tried to force himself upon a date one other time."

Mark told the probation-parole officer that since he had already told the police everything, if the officer wanted to know anything he could get his information from the police records. However, Mark told the officer that he had been married somewhere in Georgia in 1971. His "wife" said that they were never married. They do have a small child. Mark's "wife" told the officer that the charges against the subject would in no way affect her relationship and feelings toward him. She also indicated that the information Mark had given the police was entirely incorrect.

The victims' statements to the probation-parole officer for the P.S.I. were incomplete. One victim, Linda, stated that she was very much afraid of Mark and never wanted to meet with him. Of the other two victims, one had moved out of state, and Jane had moved and left no address.

Mark first came into contact with the Criminal Justice System in this state one month before his fourteenth birthday. He was arrested for breaking and entering a business establishment, and for grand larceny. *Within the next two months Mark was arrested six more times,* five for breaking and entering stores with grand larceny and vandalism, and once for being in a car that he knew had been stolen. Each of these seven arrests were for a serious felony. A felony is an offense that carries a prison sentence.

Each time Mark was arrested he was referred to the custody of the Juvenile Court. Each time, the Juvenile Court returned him to the custody of his home, on probation. His eighth arrest was made less than three months after his first arrest. This arrest was for truancy: Mark had missed forty-two of the past sixty days of school. With the eighth arrest, and with his past record, Mark was sentenced to the state reform school for boys until he reached the age of twenty-one.

In less than six months' time Mark (with the help of another inmate) had escaped from the school. This was accomplished in the following manner: As a cook from the school was driving across the campus, the two boys stepped in front of her car. The other boy put a knife to her ribs, ordered her to leave her purse on the seat and to get out of the car. This she did, whereby the two boys jumped into the car and sped off. Within a few miles of the school they wrecked the car. They jumped out and ran into the woods. Within the hour, Mark had been caught and was lodged in the county jail. He was found guilty of armed robbery and escape and was sentenced to from six months to five years in the state prison.

Mark was fifteen years old when he arrived at the state prison for first offenders. In many states, a juvenile at the age of fourteen may be sent to an adult prison if his crimes are of a very serious nature and if the reform schools do not have adequate security to control the individual or to prevent escapes.

It is a well-established fact that the earlier in life one starts serious criminal activities, the less likely is the chance of "rehabilitation." Many people argue that a criminal learns criminal traits in reform school. Juvenile court judges do their best to avoid sending *anyone* to reform school (note Mark's seven serious felony offenses). Therefore, it is only the ones who have had many previous chances to stop their criminal activities who are sent to reform schools. They developed their criminal way of life in the free world, long before they arrived at the reform school.

Mark was so incorrigible in prison that he was not paroled until he had served almost the maximum sentence. He was paroled at the age of nineteen. He completed his parole during his twentieth year. One month after his twenty-first birthday, Mark was arrested for rapes he had been committing while on parole.

When Mark was arrested in his home county, detectives in an adjoining county obtained information that Mark fitted the description given to them smack into the side of a truck on the highway. The truck didn't stop, and by a victim who had been brought to a hospital in their county. Mark's M.O. also matched the information given to them by this victim. Therefore, the detectives took a photo-pack to the victim. She immediately identified the picture of Mark as being that of her assailant. As a result, a warrant charging Mark with Rape, Battery, and Imprisonment was issued from this county. It was served on Mark in the jail where he was awaiting sentencing on the charges for which he had been arrested.

As soon as the presentence investigation was completed, and the psychiatric evaluations submitted to the Court, Mark would be sentenced for the crimes for which he had been arrested and had pled guilty. He would then be transferred to the jail in the other county to stand trial on the new charges.

The original presentence investigation made on Mark did not indicate that he would be a good probation risk, or that society would be protected if he were allowed to remain free on probation. There was his serious record of felonies committed before he was sent to reform school. There was his armed robbery and escape from reform school. And there was evidence that he had been committing rapes almost from the day he was released on parole from his first prison term.

The evaluations submitted by the two psychiatrists who examined Mark were not encouraging either. Both psychiatrists agreed that Mark suffered from a personality disorder; specifically, antisocial personality. *"His long-standing history of psychopathy and antisocial behavior* seems to have moved into a propensity to commit sexual offenses of a dangerous nature. This subject fits the criteria for the diagnosis of criminal sexual psychopath under state statutes."

Taking all things into consideration, the judge determined that Mark should serve twenty-five years on four of the charges, and five years on two of the charges. However, the sentences were to run concurrently (at the same time). This meant that instead of serving a total of one hundred and ten years, Mark would only have to serve a maximum sentence of twenty-five years. With gain time (days reduced from his sentence for good behavior) he could be totally free within seventeen years—in some states he could be free within thirteen years. He would be eligible for parole immediately after sentencing! Absurd, isn't it?

Because Mark met the criteria of a criminal sexual psychopath, the Court sentenced Mark first to the custody of the division of mental health to be placed in the sex offender treatment program.

However, before Mark would be sent to the sex offender program, it was necessary that he be transferred to the detention center in the county where he was to stand trial for the crime he had committed there.

When I was interviewing Mark in the prison he mentioned this crime to me briefly. He said, "There was this one time one got away from me and ran quite a few cars passed before anyone stopped to help her." Mark laughed.

The victim's story is not the same, nor was it amusing to her: Only one month before Nancy was assaulted in the bushes beside the interstate, sixteen-year-old Carmen barely escaped with her life from the same area.

Carmen, like Mark's other victims, had been hitchhiking from the beaches after dark. Mark stopped to pick her up, but it was not until Carmen had entered the vehicle that she discovered the driver to be the man who had picked her up approximately one week earlier from another beach, and had raped her. She hadn't reported that rape to the police. This time she realized what was coming, but it was too late. As he pulled away from the curb, Mark grabbed her hair and forced her to the floor.

Mark struck Carmen in the face when she pleaded with him to take her home. He continued to beat her with his fists and pick her back with the paint scraper intermittently while he was driving. When Mark reached his favorite spot beside the interstate, he forced Carmen out of his car, across a ditch, and into the tall bushes. Mark removed Carmen's blouse and as he kneeled to remove her skirt, Carmen broke and ran toward the interstate. Mark, infuriated, ran to his car, started it, and attempted to run over her. Carmen dove into the median strip, at that point a steep incline, to avoid being struck by Mark's vehicle. Disgusted that his prey had eluded him, Mark continued to drive northbound on the interstate.

Carmen crawled up the incline and walked onto the northbound lane, attempting to stop motorists for assistance. She was struck on the right leg by one vehicle, which proceeded on northward after knocking her to the pavement. She again went back to the roadway. After being passed by several vehicles, someone finally stopped and carried her to the hospital in the county where she had been injured.

To the probation-parole officer making the presentence investigation on Mark for this crime, Mark told still a different story from the short one he had told me. He told the officer that he picked up the victim while she was hitchhiking, that he did assault her while he was driving along the interstate, but that he did not have any plan of taking the girl to a particular area. He admitted to the officer that he had intended to rape the victim, but that she ran onto the interstate and he left in his car. Mark told the officer that he was unaware of ever seeing the girl before.

While Mark was in the county detention center awaiting further disposition of the charges of rape, battery, and imprisonment, in connection with his assaults upon Carmen, he and five other prisoners escaped from a cell block, after hacksawing a heavy steel grate covering an air vent. The prisoners climbed onto the roof and fled. Several hours later Mark was apprehended, along with one of the other escapees, and was returned to the detention center.

Regarding his escape, Mark told the probation-parole officer that he was serving a twenty-five-year sentence while being incarcerated at the detention center, and that the other inmates had hacksawed the opening in the roof. He related that the urge to escape was too strong, and that he merely exited the detention center and was apprehended several hours later. Mark pointed out that he put up no resistance at the time of being apprehended.

Mark pled guilty as charged to rape, battery, and imprisonment. He was adjudged guilty of escape. The Court remanded Mark to the custody of the division of mental health. Sentencing was deferred until such time as the defendant should be adjudged cured.

Finally, seven months after his arrest, Mark was transferred from the county jail to the sex offender treatment program at the state mental hospital. He had already been diagnosed by two private psychiatrists—who would in no way benefit from Mark's hospitalization—as having an antisocial personality disorder (being a psychopath).

During the three and a half years that Mark was kept in the hospital program, the staff—whose jobs depended upon having patients in the program for sex offenders—issued five psychiatric evaluations and recommendations. At no time did the staff evaluate Mark as psychotic. Nor would the staff admit during the first four evaluations that Mark was a psychopath. However, on the fifth and final evaluation, after three and one-half years of "treatment," the staff's final diagnosis was "personality disorder, antisocial type"—*exactly the same diagnosis made by the two private psychiatrists four years earlier.*

It was determined by the hospital staff that: "This patient (Mark) was no longer considered a menace in terms of propensity of committing sexual offenses. The staff, however, determined that because of the patient's continuous behavior of acting out, it is probable that this propensity toward other antisocial activities is still present. It is the staff's opinion that he has received maximum benefit and should be returned to court for further disposition of his case."

Mark was returned to the county where he had assaulted Carmen. Although the first Court had sentenced Mark before he was sent to the hospital for "treatment," this Court had deferred sentencing until after hospitalization.

Therefore, four years after the first presentence investigation was conducted on Mark, an updated P.S.I. was ordered. Fortunately for society, this judge was able to decipher the involved psychiatric terms used by the hospital evaluation team and included in the updated P.S.I. In essence these reports noted that Mark had matured somewhat and was getting along "as well as could be expected" for a psychopath. In other words, his long stay at the hospital will make him easier to live with in prison. In the language of the prison, Mark had picked up a case of institutionalization.

This judge determined that Mark remained a definite menace to society. For the crimes of rape, battery, and imprisonment he sentenced Mark to Life in prison. This sentencing would run concurrently with the twenty-five years sentences he was already serving. However, for the crime of escape, Mark was sentenced to five years in the state prison—to run consecutively (to start after his other sentences have been completed, or he has been paroled). Therefore, Mark's prison sentence reads: *Life plus five.*

As I talked with this rapist, after he had spent over three and one-half years in "treatment" and after he had spent a total of over ten of his twenty-six years of life in institutions, many evidences of psychopathy (antisocial personality) crept into his conversation. Statements such as, "The reason I got into trouble was because of my friends . . . I never had any trouble getting a job, it was keeping it. Sometimes one lasted two weeks, sometimes two hours, the longest nine months." Frequent job change is classic for the psychopath. "I got railroaded when I escaped from the reform school. But I had a good time while I was in state prison." Punishment to the psychopath is no more than an affront or an annoyance, since it is something he does not take seriously to heart. "The reason I started raping was because I missed so much while I was in prison." Yet he was living with a woman. "I only had one person resist me, and she got away and ran into a truck. She was the only girl who resisted me." The record speaks for itself. "I never did much Peeping Tom. I was afraid of the dark."

In answer to my question of how he justified the rapes to himself, he said, "I didn't try to justify it to myself. There was no justification at all. *I was doing what I wanted to do and that's the way it was going to be.*

Mark, who had raped at least fifty young women and possibly had murdered at least one girl, made this parting statement to me: "It's very hard to feel guilty for hurting somebody when you have no idea in the world who they were. I couldn't even tell you what they looked like. They were just people, that was it."

LARRY

"My first sexual experience was with my mother. I attempted an assault on her. The situation with my mother was premeditated, I don't know how long. I heard my dad when he left on a fishing trip. And I went in and my mother was asleep. I pulled part of the covers back and slipped my hand under the covers on to her leg. And she woke up. And of course, she was shocked. She didn't really try to resist me in the sense that she screamed or hollered or something, because I was her son. She's shocked at what's going on, and she's trying to understand what's happening. As I continued to fondle her and so forth, she kept asking, why am I doing this? why am I doing this? and so forth. And I just said, 'Be quiet, be quiet.' I slipped her nightgown up to her waist, and fondled her breasts. She let me fondle her breasts, then she said, 'That's enough.' And I remember I felt frustrated at that point, and there was nothing else. Then I asked her if she was going to say anything about it to my dad, and she said, 'Well, I don't know whether I will or not.' So I went back to my bedroom at that time. And I remember thinking, 'I've really got myself into it now.' Because I was sure she would tell my dad about it. Well, the outcome of that was that my dad threatened me with a meat cleaver and said he'd kill me if I ever touched her again. Which put a very prompt halt to my fantasizing about her."

When I interviewed him, this rapist had already received over twenty years of treatment in sex offender programs and prisons, so he talked glibly about his crimes. He was the typical psychopathic personality. He felt absolutely no guilt for any of his actions, though he talked of guilt often. Whatever he did was always someone else's fault, usually his parents' or the devil's. At no time in his interviews did this rapist ever take responsibility for any of his actions. He bragged constantly, such as "she loved me to pieces," and "he has political influence, and this goes all the way to the governor." At no time did he use violence, *he says*. But we have proof that he broke a victim's arm, when he was committing a rape only two months after he had been released on parole from fifteen years in sex offender programs and prison.

This rapist spoke fluently of the merits of various types of sex offender treatments, but he often mispronounced psychological terms. He was a nice enough looking man, in his early forties. He spoke so sincerely and so easily, that he could have easily conned a person into believing that he was cured. His record proves he was not.

This rapist speaks of an adolescence of being a Peeping Tom in his neighborhood. And of going into single women's homes by prying open a window, of taking the women's panties and bras and masturbating with them on the bed. On a few occasions, when he was in the house the women would come home. He would go out the window "in the middle of the situation," as he described it. "And have to leave everything where it was. And, of course, the police would come in and they would wonder what was going on and all." He states that if his parents ever had any suspicion of what was going on, and he is sure that on a couple of occasions they did, they never said anything about it.

As I listened to this rapist speak academically of his assaults—he rarely spoke of them as rapes—clues to his personality were present in all of his tales. Consent on the part of the victim, their consent to a sexual act, is the element most strongly contested in a rape case. I have never interviewed a rapist who has not told me that the victim consented voluntarily to have intercourse with him—even those rapists who had kidnapped their victims, or were armed with guns or knives, insisted that the victims consented voluntarily!

Using this rapist's own words where possible, I should like you to hear of some of his assaults. After so many years in prisons and sex offenders' programs it is difficult for the rapist to keep his stories accurate. But we can discern a pattern to his rapes. And on the last two rapes that we know of, we were able to verify what really happened during his assaults.

As we consider the early rapes, we must remember that they happened almost twenty-five years ago, at a time when rape was even less understood than it is today. To become pregnant without being married was a disgrace to the family. As I listened to what he referred to as his first "lust thought," I realized that he had raped the girl who was evidently forced to become his wife. The rapist says: "When I returned from Korea I had intended on going to school, finishing my junior college, then going on to a Christian college."

While visiting with a friend, the rapist met the girl who was to become his wife. "This girl and her cousin came to the house one day, one evening, and we stood up and were introduced. Nothing attractive to me about her, not the way she was dressed or anything. Nice girl, but I wasn't a bit attracted, nothing at all. And I had a very definite lust thought go through my head. She was dressed from neck to ankle with a red coat on. She had short hair and was laughing. I literally shook my head and I thought, 'I don't want that in there.' And whoosh, it was gone. It's not that I was anti-sex or anti-anything like that. I didn't have any problems in meeting girls, or with heterosexual relationships. At this point, as far as I'm concerned, whatever had been there previously had been sublimated to the point where it wasn't bothering me. It wasn't manifesting itself, it wasn't evident, and things were going along fine."

But shortly after he met this girl he went around to her apartment. She invited him into her apartment for a cup of coffee, the rapist says, "And I didn't really have any attraction to her, she was a nice girl, but no chemistry, no communication really between us. And I felt kind of sorry for her actually. So I leaned over and kissed her, and she responded. There was still nothing there, I didn't have any feeling for her really. Just this person, and I felt sorry for her, and she wasn't going out at all that I knew of. I didn't know hardly anything about her, really. So I just kind of felt sorry for her. And I kind of felt bad because I didn't want anything to get started anyway.

"But we had intercourse right away. I didn't want to and she didn't want to. I was so mad at myself. Of course, she felt bad, you know, here she was a virgin, and I was too at this point, you know, and we'd both blown the whole thing, so to speak. And I was holding myself at fault, to me it just ruined a big part of my life right there. And I was acting the way I was, and was taking it personally against her, naturally. She just happened to be involved, unfortunately, you know."

Question: "You had normal intercourse?"

Answer: "Yeah."

Question: "Did you use any violence with her at all?"

Answer: "No."

Question: "None at all?"

Answer: "None. I mean, she was crying, but she wasn't—I mean you have to remember, it wasn't an experience that she had expected any more than I had. and *it was like this lust came out again,* right? I mean, here she was, and there I was, and then that was that. And she didn't resist all that much, if at all really. I mean, she didn't know what to do, the truth about it was. It wasn't a forced situation, really forced."

Question: "Did she ask you to stop?"

Answer: "Not really. I mean, stop yes, you know, not really stop."

Question: "How did you finish?"

Answer: "Oh I don't know. We had relations three or four times. It was a relaxed thing. It was relaxed."

Question: "When did she begin to cry?"

Answer: "Oh, I said at first she was kind of crying because she was upset. But she was a full and willing participant after that. *I mean, I didn't force her, it was not a forced thing.* Definitely not a forced thing. Definitely not. A lot of times a girl realizes it's not maybe the thing she wanted to do at the time. So there it was and it was happening, so the proper response was to be a little resistive. But the reality was the resistance really wasn't there. So that's why I say it wasn't a forced situation."

Question: "Did you sleep?"

Answer: "Afterwards to rest a little. We had intercourse three or four times that night, and got up about six o'clock. We went for a ride. And I ran off at the mouth for about an hour and a half about how I had just ruined everything in my life, and hers too (at which the rapist laughs). And of course, now here she was and now she'd lost her virginity and here was this guy that was ranting and raving and hollering about how his life had been ruined by this particular experience. And this was a blow to her too, right down the line. So it was bad for both of us, you know, but she didn't say anything about when will I see you again, or anything like that. I just left her off in front, and she went up to her apartment.

"I didn't want to have anything else to do with the situation, because I didn't want it to go any further. And yet I felt sorry for her too. Here I'd stepped in and felt I'd ruined part of her life. And I just wanted to get away from the thing, yet I felt sorry for her too. I just didn't want to be so cold-blooded that I just commit a (*here he caught himself*), that we have an experience and then just never see her again.

"We had intercourse a few times after that. And then she found out she was pregnant. Of course, she was shocked. She didn't know what to do. She liked me, but she knew that I didn't love her, and I was constantly mad for being weak enough to get involved and continue that irregular type of relationship. But I said, 'Let's just wait and see what happens.' (He laughs). 'Like, what's going to happen? She's going to continue to get more pregnant. (He laughs again). So I'm looking for a way out. I don't love her. I don't want to get married under any circumstances. If I'd loved her it would have been a different story, probably. I'd have said, 'Well, maybe for the best.' But I wanted some way out of it, now what's she going to do.

"One day her mother said, 'Don't you have something to tell me.' 'Oh, Boohoohoo and so forth, you know.' 'Well, who was it?' 'Ohhhhhhh.' 'So her mother called up my mother. And my mother in no emphatic words said, '*You will* get married.' And (here he laughs) I said, 'I *will not* get married. That's all there is to it.' So my mother was very emphatic about the fact that 'you are gonna get married. That's all there is to it.' 'Well, I'm not going to get married.' My mother says then, 'I don't want to hear it.' "

The victim was willing to go to a home for unwed mothers. And the rapist felt that she had made the decision, and that's how she felt—that she saw the way he was responding, and that he was in silent agreement.

"Well, we got married in August. I was trying to go to school, and work, plus everything else involved in a marriage. She was working for awhile. And it went along pretty good, an innocent marriage, we were kind of caught up in the mechanics of all that, you know.

"But my school was falling further and further behind. Well, I was locked in now. I don't know about her. I still don't know until this day how she felt. But I didn't have a real love for her at all. I couldn't like her. She wasn't unlikable by any means (he laughs again). She was a nice girl. But there was just no attraction there.

"In December I started going out and being a Peeping Tom again. It wasn't a sexual need, by any means. It never has been. And it wasn't primarily a sexual act itself. But I started being a Peeping Tom in December.

"I got up out of bed one night. She was asleep, and of course, she's about seven months pregnant. And I got up and got dressed and went out and went down to this woman's house. And entered the house through a place where they put in coal. And I tried to attack this woman while she was sleeping. I knew she was alone—they're always alone. This was not a momentary thing. It was premeditated."

Question: "Was she already picked out?"

Answer: "Oh yeah."

He continues, "I tried to assault her and she woke up and she started screaming and yelling. And I just thought, 'Man, what am I doing?' I meant to have sexual intercourse with her. O.K. She was sleeping and she turned over. I was crouching down by the side of the bed, and the heater was on, and it gave out a little light. And when she turned over in her sleep she must have sensed somebody's presence. She just opened her eyes and she caught a glimpse of me crouched down beside the bed, and that's when she started yelling.

"So I tried to put my hand over her mouth to try to quiet her and she started struggling and kicking and everything. She was pretty athletic. I just stopped and tried to get out of the house, but there was no door to get out because all the doors were locked. And I wasn't going out the way I came in, so she stood out there in the room and she was very hoarse. And of course, she was in a state of shock to some degree, and she was demanding that I get out of the house.

"And here I am trying to get the doors open. And finally I stopped and opened the door and ran home. My wife was up, standing in the door when I came in. She was shocked when I came running into the house. And I thought by this time the lady whose house I had been in would have called the police. It was only about a block and a half away from our apartment. And my wife said, 'Where you been?' And I said, 'Don't worry about it. Go to bed. I'll be in in a minute.' She didn't say anything, she just couldn't understand what was going on I guess. That was the only indication that something was going on, something overt. She didn't say a word about it."

Question: "You said you already had this lady picked out?"

Answer: "I always had a definite plan. Maybe I had been observing her house and her for about two weeks. She didn't know me. None of my victims ever knew me. I knew about them only through observation. Not all the time. Sometimes it would just be a momentary thing. In most cases it had been premeditated observation and Peeping Tom and planning."

Question: "When the woman struggled you didn't hurt her?"

Answer: "Well I tell you. I had my hands over her mouth—I had my left hand on her neck and my right hand over her mouth and she was struggling, she was pretty strong. And the bed was right next to a window. And I got to thinking, 'If she starts to kicking too much she might kick the window out.' But she wouldn't be quiet. She wasn't going to be passive about this whatsoever. And she was struggling and kicking and I wasn't in a position to stop her without hurting her. I mean really doing some harm to her and all, other than what I was already doing, under the shock of what she was going through. I never hurt them like cutting them with a knife or beating them or something like that, I never hurt them." Yet we have proof that he did injure his victims physically as well as emotionally. "She was under this state of shock, and she was trying to struggle to get out from under this. She's mad, I mean, she wasn't a passive female. She was mad about what was going on, and she wasn't about to let anything happen. She was going to run me out of the house. And she did.

"But I did not—uh, O.K. I put my hand over her mouth and I was pressing kind of hard, and I had this part of my hand and my thumbs were down around her throat. My left hand was behind her neck. And I didn't have her neck in my hand, I wasn't choking her, because I was pressing down with my right thumb and pushing up with my left thumb, so I wasn't putting any pressure on her neck, really. Now when you're in the middle of something like that you don't really know how much pressure you're putting on, because your adrenalin runs so fast, so you can do somebody some harm physically and not really know you're doing it, actually. And not really intend to. I'm just saying I was not physically inflicting pain upon her, in order to make her submit. I was just trying to make her be quiet. Well she wasn't going to be quiet, so I got up and ran."

Question: "You went into that house without planning an escape route? Why? Most rapists unlock a door before they awaken the person, so that they will be able to make a fast exit."

Answer: "Because I wasn't planning on it being unsuccessful."

This rapist tells of another rape that was committed about two months later. This was in February, while his wife was in the hospital giving birth to their baby. Like most of his victims, this was an older woman who lived by herself. The rapist . . . "had been in her place many times when she wasn't there. It was kind of a motel made into apartments. I just looked through her things. I went into her house about ten times, over a period of weeks and weeks and weeks. She worked in the daytime. I got in through the back door. It was always unlocked. She lived in the very back of the court. Probably thought she was quite safe.

"These assaults didn't always start out as being a sexual thing. They were for the thrill of the moment. It may have come out a sexual thing in the end, but not to start with.

"In most of my offenses it was very difficult to get an erection. Very difficult. Even if they submitted quietly. Because I was under tremendous strain. In my last two offenses there was no erection. One lasted from seven o'clock in the evening til twelve o'clock at night. There was an oral offense that took place in that one, but there was no erection and no ejaculation."

The rapist continues to tell about this rape: "In this particular situation, when the offense did occur, and there was no sexual assault, I stopped and I thought, 'God, here I am again. And I got a robe for her, yellow chintz, got a robe for her, and sat her down on the bed, and asked her if I could talk to her.

"Of course, she was shaking like crazy, and she said, 'Go ahead,' like whatever you want to do, 'cause I was in charge of everything, you know. And I talked to her.

"And I said, 'Look, I don't want to do this. I don't want to be doing it.' I started crying, I said, 'I'm married, my wife's in the hospital having a baby right now. And I'm out doing this?' I don't understand why I'm doing it. I said, 'I've read some of your—now she had had problems with her marriage, and she had been going to a psychiatrist and a dream analyist, and all kinds of stuff, even hypnosis, and writing it down. —And she said, 'Oh yeah!' That was more shocking to her than what had just occurred. My reading anything about her life. She said, 'Oh you shouldn't have done that!'

"But I told her, I said, 'I wish we could come over and talk to you.' Of course, she was agreeable to anything at that point," he laughs. "So I said, 'I'm sorry for what happened. I don't know what's going to happen to me.' We just sat there. And I said, 'Are you alright?' And I just ran out through the back door."

Then the rapist continues to speak to me, sounding as though he was committing many more rapes than he is admitting: "My M.O. was developing along the way, but I would try not to leave any fingerprints or anything. At this point, as I'm starting out, or restarting, I'm really not that con wise to all the little ends and outs about police evidence and getting caught. I'm not privy to all the little things I need to do to not leave myself open to not getting arrested. I became more cautious, but I didn't get professional with it. I wouldn't go into a house as a burglar, I would go in as a sexual offender. And I left things in the same order that I found them. It was a Breaking and Entering even though it was motivated by something else. See, the same thing occurred in another case that summer.

"This was one case where there was no premeditation, no pre-investigation, no pre-observatory. I saw her walking on the street, and I just followed her home. And she went to pick up her mail, and I parked the car and walked right past her at the mailbox and walked right up to her apartment. Not knowing her or if she lived with anybody or anything else. It was uncanny how many of these cases (his rapes), and the victims I was involved with—the ones I had not observed, that I never had seen before, were living alone and in what with my M.O. I considered an acceptable type of environment. That is an environment which is susceptible to attack.

"On two occasions women driving down the street, and it was dark and I could only see the back of their heads, and yet I would lock into that, and follow her. And that person would be the type, generally speaking, that would attract me. Because many didn't attract me. But they were the kind that I would have committed an assault with—an offense with. And they would be living alone, and would be living in circumstances that would fit my M.O. that would be ideal. And it was really uncanny. You see, I would not assault a younger girl in her twenties or anything like that. They were always older women. Almost every one of my cases it was an older woman. Between forty and sixty." (The rapist was in his twenties during these rapes.)

His last two cases were in their late fifties or early sixties. At this time he was forty. "All of my offenses have been against older women. My mother's age. It was definitely directed toward the mother image. No doubt about that. I know that psychologically a lot of it was directed toward her. The thing that bothers me is that in all my years of therapy I can't find anything in my early life. Freudly (sic) speaking these things are supposed to be developed.

"All except one woman I know of reported it. In the cases involved I could have gotten shot, or blown away, many times. But it never occurred. They were always safe, it's amazing. Later on I confessed to everything I could think of.

"Here I was out doing this while my wife's in the hospital having a baby. So you can see where our relationship was. It wasn't very far."

The rapist now tells of another incident that he says happened many, many times. "I was sitting on the bench in front of her door, and she came around to the side and she looked at me sitting there, and I said something about the sunset or something. She was suspicious, you know. She walked around to her door and I got up and she was kind of fumbling for her key. She knew something was going to happen. So she finally did get the key in the door, which she shouldn't have done," the rapist says. "I mean—that's another thing. If there is somebody hanging around like that, the first thing she should have done was simply walk two feet across that little hall and knock on the door across the hall. Or fumble with her key at that apartment, or something. Because that wasn't even her apartment, and maybe there would be somebody there who would have helped her. Or if she had just walked right down the stairs when she finds a stranger there. She should not have stood there and opened her door while I was standing right there. In fact, I was surprised when she did it, as wary as she was at that moment.

"So anyway, I grabbed her from behind, put my hand over her mouth, and she fell down. I got her inside the apartment and closed the door. And I bound and gagged her, which was my usual M.O. I would usually do that, put something in her mouth, a stocking or something, and then wrap around it. I would get these things in the apartment.

"After I bound and gagged her I looked around the apartment some. And then the phone rang. And then I attempted sexual assault. But I couldn't get an erection. I always assaulted the victim vaginally. Except the last one. On the last one it would have been vaginal also if I had been able to get an erection. That last victim actually initiated that (fellatio) to some degree, because the thought running in both of our minds was that if I did and reached a climax, can I go. And of course, she was willing to get rid of me one way or the other.

"Anyway, to go back to that particular girl in the apartment house. After I had done everything I could to get her and couldn't then I sat there and I looked at her and I looked at the situation and I thought, once again, like I come to myself, and I said, 'Well'—and she had been looking at me much of the time, and this was in the daylight. So I sat there on the edge of the bed and I said, 'Well,' I said. 'I don't know what's going to happen here. But I'm going to untie you and ungag you and put your robe on. And you can call the police and you can do what you want to do.'

"This assault had been going on and on. So she sat up and she got herself composed, somewhat, and once again I told her—and I'm talking to her rationally now, I'm telling her about my wife and baby, who's about five months old. And if she wants to call the police she can call them. Or she can sit there or whatever she wants to do.

"And she felt sorry for me, you know. I told her I'd like to bring my wife over. And she said, 'Well I wish you'd do that. I need to have somebody to talk to!' And she was some kind of secretary. Now she actually said, 'Well look, I want you to make me a promise that you'll never do this again,' you know, and so forth. And I said, 'Well I don't want to but I'm not going to promise that it's not going to happen. Because I can't control it.' And she was about twenty one and she was a virgin at this point. And she took me and she hugged me and she said, 'Now I want you to promise me that you'll come over. To call ahead of time and bring your wife over, and we'll try to talk about it,' you know. And I walked out slowly.

"But about two weeks later she saw an incident in the paper, and a description fit me. And she knew right then it was me. So she told a girlfriend of hers who had a boyfriend that was a policeman. And that's how it got reported."

Question: "You're doing this kind of regularly. Did you do anything other than tying the women up? Did you do anything like beating them?"

Answer: "In three cases I did hit them in the stomach, with my fist. This was to knock the wind out of them. It wasn't ever a real vicious blow. This was to keep them quiet. I hadn't gagged them yet. This was like on the initial assault, if I wasn't in a position to cover their mouth or something. Then there might be a struggle in which they would be yelling or something. So I would eliminate the yelling right off the bat by hitting them in the stomach to knock the wind out of them. But it was never a real vicious blow that would maybe have broken a rib or something. It was just so they couldn't get their breath so they would be quiet until I could get in a position where they wouldn't make a noise. I didn't do anything vicious or anything like that."

Now the rapist starts to generalize: "It's getting more and more frequent, and in the daytime. Like one time I was driving down the street about ten o'clock in the morning. I was in sales work—never had a problem at my job. You've heard the expression of a monkey on your back? Well, this thing was sitting on my shoulder, and it said, 'O.K. let's go. Let's go out and find one.' Twice I was surrounded by police. They were all over the place. And I jumped or climbed walls that I couldn't possibly have climbed without the adrenalin being up. There was this one apartment that I walked up and down in front of it for about an hour and a half. And then I went in and got this woman tied up and was half way through when I stopped and ran out. I ran down the railroad tracks, and police were all over, and I got away. But that lady was so torn up she had to take a six-months' leave from her job—in fact, she had a nervous breakdown over it."

This rapist was finally arrested. He states that he pleaded guilty, and that his sentence was a three years to life sentence. This meant his first parole date was one year after being sentenced. But he was kept in that state's prisons and sex offender program for fifteen years.

Only two months after his parole he was arrested for rape in another state. He was again sent to a sex offender program, where he stayed for four years—during which time he became engaged to marry one of the church visitors! From the sex-offender program this rapist was sentenced to ten years in a state prison.

Verification is possible on the two rapes the rapist committed after spending fifteen years in confinement. The rapist tells about these rapes:

"I had some idle time and these thoughts started to come back. Exactly the same way they had happened fifteen years ago. Just exactly. Same M.O. and everything, and I went for it.

"I saw this nice looking elderly woman walking down the street. And I had this same feeling, something just locked me in. I followed her home and she lived by herself. When I first saw her I went for her. Then when she went into the house I stopped.

"But on Saturday I had worked overtime, and when I finished I was just riding around, and I saw this lady walking down the street. And I knew how far she had to go. So I turned the car around and asked her if she wanted a ride. And she said, 'No thank you. I only have a couple of blocks to go.' So she went on and turned the corner. And I went down and parked my car right in the open less than a block away. It was a big car with out of state license plates. And I was completely possessed by this thing.

"I ran back to the house. She was kicking a can out of the street. I went back in the back of the house. She had heavy screens in the windows and she had like a grill type wrought iron on the windows. The place was secure. It was still daylight. And when I was at the back door she was still getting into the front door. Well, I tried to get the back door open and I pulled it almost off the hinges. I mean I was just berserk. And that made a racket, pulling that back. But the screen door did come open. And there was another door with a big glass in it. And it was locked too. I'm frantic at this point. So I broke the glass—which, of course, cut me up. And there was blood and everything. The glass shattered over everything. But I couldn't get that door open.

"So I ran out the back, after all this noise, and I come around the front. And my hand's bleeding and everything. And she was just going in the front door. She was looking toward the back, and I guess she was putting the keys back in her purse. And I just opened the screen door, put my hand around her mouth—not the hand that was cut—from behind her, and she didn't struggle or anything.

"She was shocked. In my mind I fully intended to commit a rape. It was right back, *I just picked up where I left off* what was going on. My hand was bleeding, so with that same hand I tried to put my handkerchief around it to stop the bleeding.

"She has a divan, a two-seat, real small divan. So anyway I was trying to get her over there. I wanted to gag her so she wouldn't yell out. I had no intention so to speak, you know. I didn't do any physical damage to her, so to speak. I got her over by the couch and then she started really fighting back, resisting. And there was no way she was going to let me gag her, that was all there was to it. So I didn't. She had a pair of glasses on and I tried to get the glasses off. She didn't want to take her glasses off.

"I was talking to her all this time, trying to get her to calm down. Finally she calmed down somewhat. Then the phone rang, because one of the neighbors had heard all this racket going on. Busting glass and everything else. Somebody called up, so when the phone rang she was standing right there. She was looking right at me. She kept looking at me. So I looked at her and I thought, 'Boy here I am again. This is it.' I said, 'Answer it, but don't tell them what's going on.' So she picked up the phone, and of course she was shaking. But she was pretty well under control at that point. Somebody asked her if everything was alright. He asked her, 'Are you O.K. over there?' And she said, 'Yes.' He asked her a couple of questions, and finally he said, 'Are you sure everything is alright?' And she said, 'No.' I was listening through the earpiece. And I thought, 'Oh boy.' And I said, 'Now I gotta run.'

"Then I took the receiver out of her hand and I hung it up. And I thought if I just run she might start screaming or yelling or something. Which I don't think she would. At that point I think she was too shocked or scared or something. Cause she hadn't tried to do that prior to that. So I turned around and I hit her in the solar plexis. Just enough, and she went down on the floor.

She doubled up. She wasn't hurt or anything like that, it just knocked the wind out of her. So I ran. I ran out the front door, and I ran right out in the middle of the street right down to my car. Nobody came out. I didn't see anybody anywhere. And I was expecting somebody to come. So I started the car up and I took off.

"I drove around a while. I even went by her place. I never saw any police or anything. And I said, 'Boy, I got out of that.' I didn't know what to do. I didn't have enough money saved up to leave. So I went back to my apartment and I cleaned up. Then I went to a drug store and got something for my hand. And I went back to my apartment and read a little and went to bed.

"And the next incident didn't happen until two or three weeks after that. About two and a half." Actually, his next rape occurred in three days.

His Last Victim: "I saw her one time, and here it was, that's the one. Lived all by herself. No prior observation. I knew well what I was doing, but I yielded to it. I just saw her get out of the car and I said, that's the one. I didn't know anything about her. I saw where she went in, and I went to the back of the house and looked in the window and saw that she was the one that was in there. The house was beside a big vacant lot, and it was after dark, and I just stood there looking in the window. It was strange, all of the victims lived alone.

"She came into the bedroom and she looked over at the window. I was staring through the window right at her. And so I just ran to my car.

"About two or three nights later, I parked right there by the window. I'm sitting on the driver's side. And it was dark in the room. Her car wasn't in its parking place by her shop so I figured she was gone. I just sat there, and I happened to look over at the window and she was at the window and she was looking right at me. And you know, she still hasn't called the police! She happened to come over and pull the curtains shut. I guess she had come in while I was sitting there. But she's standing right there looking at me and at the car, and she never called the police. This is a small town and the police are almost right across the street. This happened after she had already seen somebody looking in her window. And I started up the car and drove off, while she's looking at me. That's twice now within a week. And she still didn't call the police. She should have.

"I observed her and knew that her house was behind her shop. And that she got off work about 5:30 or 6:00. And that she would leave as soon as she came out of her shop. Then she would always come back in about an hour. So I just figured it out in my mind that I was going to enter this house and commit a rape. That's what my motive was.

"I saw her leave, so I parked my car about a block away and came back and took the bars off the window. There was nothing to the bars, they came right off. Then I went in through the window. I stayed behind a door and she came in and walked right past me. I came up behind her and grabbed her and put my hand over her mouth. She had something wrong with her back, so when I got her down on the floor and put my hand around her on her mouth she tried to relax as much as she could. She wasn't struggling at all.

"I didn't want her to get a look at my face. So I told her if she didn't say anything I would take my hand off her mouth. She told me then that she had a bad back. Then I felt her back and I could feel something wrong with her back. She told me she'd cooperate. She would do anything I wanted, just not to hurt her. That was about seven o'clock and it went on until about 12:30. And I was never able to get an erection. We talked about a lot of things. I told her the story of my life."

Question: "Was she sympathetic?"

Answer: "No."

Question: "Frightened?"

Answer: "No. She was very, very—she realized at that point I wasn't going to hurt her. She used her head. She realized, 'poor guy, he's in bad shape. He needs help real bad, but I'm in no condition to help him. At this point I've got to get out of this thing with my life.' So all along the way she did little things to leave evidence. I kept telling her I knew what she was doing. Like when I got a glass of water she tried to get me to touch the glass.

"Morally I would never touch a prostitute. And I would never get involved with a woman on a one-to-one basis. Commit adultery?—it would never happen. I just didn't go for that. And yet this has happened. And I told her I just don't understand.

"I never had an erection, though we tried every way.

"Finally it was 12:30 and I knew she had to go to work the next day. And I had to go to work the next day. Course the next day didn't get there, for me anyway. I asked her, 'Are you going to be alright?' And she said, 'Well, I'm pretty shook up. But after two or three days I'll be O.K.' And when I put her robe on she was just slowly but surely easing me out. She had very much presence of mind. After she knew she wasn't in any real danger, I mean she didn't feel like she was, not overtly anyway, then she was able to handle herself much better.

"I left her out the front door. In fact we hugged each other mutually when I walked out the door. And then she slammed the door."

And then the rapist started musing. "It's strange what goes on in a person's mind," he said. "You're looking for communication, compatability, or something, and even as gross and as abnormal as wrong as that all is, if you find any little bit of it you take it as normal. Which is what I did. She had said, 'Don't worry, I'm not going to call the police.' And I thought at the time, well I believe it. I did. I believed it because she hadn't called the police two times before. I told her I was the man looking in her window, and the man in the parked car. People should immediately report a Peeping Tom to the police and to their neighbors. You've got to have neighborhood and block communication. The police cannot handle everything that is happening. So you've got to have more communication between individual citizens. And another thing, even though she walked out to the kitchen to get some water she never had a chance to escape. It is very unrealistic for the police to think a victim can get away. She wasn't able to escape because she couldn't run fast enough. Unless she knows she can run very fast and get the door open when she gets there, she had better not try it. We had a very relaxed situation. I mean, I would get up and walk around the house sometimes. But she never had a chance to get away.

"So when I walked out of her house I just walked slowly to my car. And she didn't call the police. She called a friend of hers and he called the police immediately. I drove off and went to my apartment and went to bed. And about 3:30 that morning here they came."

We have heard the rapist's version of his crimes. Most of his rapes occurred over twenty years ago. We have only the rapist's word on what happened. However, we know his statements that none of his victims were injured are false, for his own words refute this.

Remember the time elapsed between his two arrests for rape—fifteen years in sex offender programs and prisons. Remember that he had been out of prison less than two months when he was arrested again for rape—a rape using the same M.O. that he had used fifteen years before!

A psychiatrist makes this statement: "We really don't know the cause of sexual dysfunction or sexual deviancy. All we can do is theorize. The term 'sexual offender' itself is a legal term. It is not a medical, psychiatric or psychological term. In Kinsey's book the group called 'sex offenders' confirms statistically that the average pedophiliac (child molester), exhibitionist, and other sexual deviants are *not* mentally ill. So what do we do with the sexual offender? We offer them *services:* psychological and counseling services, but I would *not* call them *treatment*, because treatment really means amelioration of symptoms and possibly cure."

A prison psychiatrist has said, "Everybody wants sex offender programs, but *I have yet to see any that will convince me that they are effective. I think that the professional who is willing to take the risk of predicting the future behavior of a sex offender is either naive or foolish.*"

For his last two rapes this rapist was *again* sent to a sex offender program, where he stayed for four years. When discharged from that program he was returned to the county where he had committed the rapes, to be sentenced for the crimes. He could have been paroled again, which often happens. Before sentencing there is an investigation into the crime, when facts about the criminal, the victims, and many other factors are recorded to help the judge reach a decision. From this same rapist's record, compiled by a very astute parole officer, we obtain an insight into the suffering of his victims.

It was the second victim the rapist assaulted who led to his arrest. A police officer observed a vehicle leaving the area of the crime with its lights out. The officer did not know a crime had been committed. But he did note the license number to see if it was a stolen vehicle. The report was negative on a stolen vehicle. But through this license number the suspect was traced to his residence, where he was arrested.

The police record reveals that the criminal gagged the victim, bound her hands, and blindfolded her. He then took her into the bathroom where he removed her clothing and took her to the bedroom where, for over five hours, the criminal forced the victim to commit fellatio upon him and in return, he committed cunnilingus upon her in an effort to acquire an erection so he could rape her.

Hear now what the parole officer has to say about the victim of this crime: "This officer contacted Mrs. X. Due to the nature of the crime and the amount of elapsed time since the crime (over four years), this officer was originally reluctant to contact the victim, however did so as instructed. Mrs. X at first stated she had almost forgotten the incident and stated that she hopes no one else has to go through the crime. She states that she tried to forget the incident and felt that the defendant should be kept off the streets. Mrs. X was extremely upset and stated that she would rather not be called on again on this crime.

"This officer would like to add his observations of this interview. When Mrs. X answered the door at her shop she appeared to be a self-confident, middle-aged business woman. However, this appearance was quickly shed when this officer revealed the nature of the business. And by the time this officer had left, Mrs. X had deteriorated to a trembling, quivering, fearful, emotional human wreck. She was extremely emotionally distraught, and it would be well-advised that she would not again have to suffer the remembrance of this crime.

"While this officer has little qualms over serving a Capias (an arrest warrant) for Violation of Probation, or even seeing someone arrested for a commission of a crime, it affects this officer greatly to see an innocent victim of the nature of Mrs. X. This officer doubts that Mrs. X will ever recover from this incident."

Let us now consider the other victim. When arrested for the rape of Mrs. X, the rapist confessed to an attempted rape three days before. The police complaint (report) on the attempted rape of Mrs. Y notes that the criminal put a sock around her throat and in her mouth. The report also notes that there was a large amount of blood on the floor and wall in Mrs. Y's house.

The parole officer also interviewed Mrs. Y. "Victim, Mrs. Y, stated that she was not sexually assaulted, although she was injured in the Assault and Battery. She stated that her arm was broken and that she was in a cast for six weeks. Mrs. Y had monetary losses for doors, locks, and screens as well as for medical expenses."

In his analysis the parole officer states: "The great amount of damage done to these women cannot be expressed in dollars, as it is more of an emotional state. Mrs. Y lives in a quasi-fortress and is extremely cautious in dealing with strangers at her door. This officer noted the extreme number of locks on each door and the presence of burglar bars, plus other means of residential security. Victim, Mrs. X, suffers even more traumatically, as she was actually sexually assaulted and bears the psychological scars of these assaults."

Appendix 2

Notes for the Professional

1. A NOTE FOR PHYSICIANS: HOW TO TESTIFY AT A RAPE TRIAL

Rape is one of the least understood of all crimes. Although it is classified as a sex crime, rape is in reality a crime of assault and violence, with sex being a component.

Most physicians do not see the victims of rape-homicide. Almost all of these victims suffer severe beatings, strangling, or fatal knife or gunshot wounds. It is not uncommon to find mutilation of the victim's breasts and genitalia, usually with a sharp instrument, in sexual assault-murder cases.

According to the F.B.I.'s Uniform Crime Reports for 1975, nearly 8 percent of all homicides are related to rape and sex offenses.

The primary feeling expressed by most rape victims is that of fear—fear of physical injury, mutilation, and death. One rape victim said, "It's not what is happening below your waist, but what is happening in your head that's so terrible."

The crime of rape is rarely recognized as a medical emergency; therefore, few hospital emergency rooms have developed standard operating procedures for rape victims. One of the outstanding rape treatment centers in the nation has been founded by and is under the direction of Dorothy J. Hicks, M.D., at Jackson Memorial Hospital, Miami, Florida, 33136. With Dr. Hicks' permission, her excellent procedure booklet is reproduced in Chapter 3.

Records of every forensic examination can be expected to be used in a potential court case. With all of the misunderstandings about the crime of rape, one needs to be as positive in one's language as possible. The physician must always remember that under the discovery laws of most states the defense attorney receives copies of all written reports, including the physician's, and also may have access to the physician's informal notes and comments.

During the physical examination of the victim, one must be careful to get good clear pictures of any bite marks, for the rapist's teeth can be matched to these bite marks. It is possible that this can be the most powerful evidence in the case. Police will be able to assist in taking these pictures.

The breast development of a young victim is also very important. By the time the case comes to court the victim may have developed physically, so that the jury sees a "woman"—perhaps a provocative one.

Note any peculiar odors about the victim or her clothing. This is good corroborating evidence if the victim has reported, or later remembers and reports to the police, a peculiar odor about the rapist or about the scene of the crime.

If the patient-victim has been a sexually active female and at the time of the examination her vagina is edematous, this should be noted. This too is excellent corroborating evidence.

A timely, believable, consistent history is necessary and must be correlated to the victim's emotional response whenever no signs of victim-resistance are found. Standing alone it may not be entitled to great weight, but in conjunction with a victim's testimony, medical-legal corroboration can be as persuasive in the minds of jurors as laboratory tests. In fact, the absence of these physical findings frequently detracts from the credibility of the victim's testimony at the trial. Many times victims are "examined" by physicians who take only evidence for the crime lab. These physicians never look at the body of the victim for such signs of trauma as grip marks on the upper arms and neck, or bruises on the thighs—common signs of a struggle with attempts at vaginal penetration.

Ours is an adversary system of law, which simply stated means, which side can sell the jury into believing their story? Therefore, pre-trial preparation is very important. A review of all of the medical notes on this patient-victim is mandatory, as is a thorough review of any deposition one has given in regard to this rape victim.

About one-third of jurisdictions permit the use of depositions in criminal matters, and they can be great time-savers to physicians. But it is much more effective to have the physician, or the nurses who assisted with this patient, testify positively during the trial itself.

Depositions are taken under oath, and can be used in open court. Therefore, they are as binding upon one as the trial. Sometimes prosecutors use a deposition instead of calling the physician to court. The defense attorney can also take a deposition from the physician about the rape victim. One of the reasons that a deposition is taken is to try to impeach and discredit the witness. Therefore, the defense attorney is the enemy. He is taking the deposition to trap the witness at the trial. Answer these questions as briefly as possible.

The physician should testify at the trial and elavorate there on the issues to help the jury understand the trauma that the victim has suffered. If the deposition is given to the prosecutor in lieu of the physician's appearing in court, the testimony at the deposition should be elaborated upon.

Another enemy of the physician-witness before and during the trial is the defense attorney, who may be a social friend. One must beware of speaking in confidence to this attorney about the case, for he may use whatever has been confided to him to discredit the witness during testimony.

Pretrial preparation also means discussing the case with the nurses who were present during the examination. Nurses make excellent witnesses to corroborate a physician's testimony. Nurses may also be used as witnesses during the trial, in lieu of physicians testifying.

If possible, one should try to get information about the rape case and the rapist from the law enforcement agency handling the case. An overall picture will put the witness in a better position to avoid being trapped by the defense attorney. However, instead of worrying about what is going to happen on cross-examination, one should try to find out what is going to happen on direct examination. It is permissible to request prosecutors to ask physician-witnesses to tell, in their own words, what was found during the initial medical examination of the victim and at subsequent follow up consultations with the victim. Most victims of rape will require short-term medical and long-term emotional support.

Another type of pre-trial preparation is that made with the prosecutor regarding the physician's arrival at the courtroom. The local medical society should arrange in advance, as standard operating procedure with the prosecutor, to allow physician-witnesses to testify either when they arrive at the courtroom, or shortly thereafter, or allow physicians to be summoned shortly before their testimony is required. The physicians will be able to testify much more positively. An angry physician, impatient with long delays and wasted time, is not the effective witness that a prosecutor needs in a rape case.

Juries are often ambivalent in their feelings toward physician-witnesses. Some jurors are in awe of them and others may be on the defensive, wondering if the physician is going to talk either over their heads or down to them. Each profession has its own language, and medical language is not the easiest to understand. Instead of using medical terms, the physician-witness should try to speak to the jury as though they are friends, not medical colleagues. The witness should explain the procedures and findings in everyday language directly to the jury. They should make the jurors a part of their discoveries. This technique, of friend speaking to friend, will also help to put the witness at ease and make the witness feel more confident. Thus the witness will be better prepared psychologically for cross-examination, if there is any, since this technique often makes cross-examination self-defeating.

To testify positively physician-witnesses may also have to explain what was *not* found. The following are examples of positive testimony:

The prosecutor could ask, "Doctor, in your opinion did this woman suffer trauma?" And the physician-witness could say, "Yes," as he had at the deposition. Or he could elaborate, "I know she suffered trauma, both physical and mental. My initial examination revealed many scratches and bruises on her body. Following the rape the patient developed an infection both in her vagina and in her mouth that was not present at the initial examination. Although she appeared calm during my examination and the police questioning, when I saw her two days later she cried so much that it was difficult for me to talk with her, etc. I also have been treating and counseling the victim and her family for the past four months—ever since the rape occurred." Both answers are truthful, but the latter is much more impressive to the jury, as well as threatening to the defense attorney.

TO POSITIVELY REPORT NEGATIVE RESULTS:

"The fact that I found no sperm present in the vaginal area is not surprising. There are many reasons that could account for this, not the least of which is the high percentage of sexual dysfunction among rapists, etc." Or, "The patient felt so dirty and defiled that immediately after she escaped from the rapist she douched and bathed and tried to wash her attacker away. It will be a long time before she will feel clean again." Or, "Although I did not see the patient before the rape, her I.U.D. (explain this and its use) was out of place. It takes a great deal of force to dislodge an I.U.D."

As a witness be calm, cool, and courteous. Rape is an emotionally laden issue. Most jurors are conscientious persons who wish to do the best possible job. The manner in which the physician-witness presents evidence may be a deciding factor in whether the jury can feel comfortable with a verdict which they must all agree upon.

2. A NOTE FOR PROSECUTORS

The Polk County Rape/Sexual Assault Care Center of Des Moines, Iowa, was funded through a federal grant. It is one of twenty programs that has earned the National Institute of Law Enforcement and Criminal Justice's "Exemplary" label. An assistant Polk County Attorney, Karla J. Fultz, who was a special prosecutor for sex crimes, makes suggestions to help those prosecuting rapists in *How to Convict a Rapist.* Many of the tasks expected of a prosecutor have been, in this book, assigned to law enforcement officers or to the victims of rape. For if they do not fulfill these tasks, they will not be done. However, most of the following suggestions can be executed only by prosecutors. Only areas that apply to all states will be included.

Depositions: You should take the time to talk with any persons to be deposed prior to the deposition. Explain carefully to each of them the reason for the deposition. It should be explained to the victim prior to this deposition that any questions in regard to her prior sexual conduct will be objected to by the prosecutor and that she should not answer these questions. Allow the victim to refresh her memory about statements given to the police at the time of the incident, and before the deposition. Explain the use of depositions as discovery, and for the purpose of impeachment.

Motions In Limine: An important trial tool for the prosecutor can be a motion in limine, which can be used to exclude any mention of the victim's prior sexual conduct on grounds of the Federal Rape Victim's Privacy Act. It can alert the court to the necessity of an in-camera hearing for such matters. It can limit defense counsel's ability to inquire into areas which can be damaging to the victim's credibility but have no bearing on the issues of the charge. Examples of this may be the presence of venereal disease in the victim, illegitimate children, or an unconventional lifestyle.

Admissibility of Other Crimes: Evidence of other crimes is admissible if it casts light on the character of the act under investigation showing either *motive, intent, absence of mistake, common scheme, identity, or a system or general pattern of criminality* so that the evidence of such other crimes would have a relevant or material bearing upon some essential aspect of the offense then being tried, except where the evidence is relevant *solely* to prove bad character or propensity.

A significant number of rapists and child molesters will have convictions of a similar offense. Each state has developed a line of cases which has allowed the introduction into evidence of crimes of a similar nature. *Evidence of similar crimes need not involve a conviction or even a charge,* but must be sufficiently clear that there is no room for speculation in the mind of the jury.

The evidence of other crimes is weighted as to its probable value versus the probability of undue prejudice. When defense counsel has interjected reputation type language into his opening statement, arguing the fact that it is a rationale for the evidence being allowed may be successful. Despite the problems, the use of such evidence is particularly useful in the prosecution of cases where consent is an issue.

Instructions: The lawyer who tries primarily civil cases will generally go to court with instructions drafted even before the jury is picked. Most prosecutors are not so well-prepared. Particularly in the trial of rape cases, advance preparation of the instructions is very important. Recent changes in the statutory and case law make many old instructions incorrect. (Misunderstandings concerning these new laws have resulted in many sentences that were much shorter than the jury had intended.)

A great deal of time and energy is expended by authorities at the time a rape is reported in trying to determine whether the rape is a "true rape" or an "unfounded allegation." This ingrained attitude of suspicion toward the victims of rape was first expressed by Lord Chief Justice Matthew Hale, the famous seventeenth-century English jurist, who wrote: "Rape is an accusation easily to be made and hard to be proved, and harder to be defended by the party accused, tho never so innocent."

Let us examine the cruel hoax Lord Hale has perpetrated upon rape victims for over 300 years, for that cautionary instruction still affects the lives of females.

At the end of each trial, before the jury goes into seclusion to deliberate on the evidence presented, the judge will read his "instructions" (sometimes called the "charge") to the jury. These instructions merely consist of an interpretation of the law and the rules of evidence as they apply to the particular case. In the case of rape trials, for the past 300 years judges have read Lord Hale's "cautionary instruction" to the jury. In California the cautionary instruction reads, "Rape is a charge which is easily made and once made is difficult to defend against, even if the person accused is innocent. Therefore, the law requires that you examine with caution the testimony of the person alleged to have been raped." *No other crime requires this cautionary instruction.*

Not until 1975 did the California Supreme Court hold that the cautionary instruction was an anachronism in California law and should no longer be given. The Court held that: *The illogic of the instruction is apparent when one considers that the same victim's testimony was untrustworthy in a rape case but was accorded the highest credibility in a robbery* (People v. Rincon-Pineda, 14 Calif, 3rd 864). In other words, the jury in this case didn't believe that the victim had been raped, but they did believe that she had been robbed! This type of illogical thinking is so common that many prosecutors routinely subject rape victims to two trials if there are two charges that can be made against the rapist.

The Lord Hale instruction which began "a charge of rape is easy to make" has been stricken down by many states. However, in its place many states have passed laws which are slanted in much the same fashion. They contain such phrases as: "If a woman consents in the least during any part of the act of intercourse, there is no such opposing will as the law requires." *In no other crime is such an instruction given.* The law would certainly never instruct a jury that if a person was accosted at gun point and asked for their money, that when they voluntarily handed it over, that they were consenting to the robbery.

Trial: It is impossible to write a "How to" article on how to try any case, civil or criminal. However, trying sex crimes is different from the trial of other crimes. *Most persons have difficulty viewing them as crimes of violence but tend to interpret them as sexual acts.*

Jury selection must be done with the knowledge that rape and other crimes involving sexual acts engender strong responses in prospective jurors. The attitude of jurors to sex crimes is generally that of disbelief. Juries given the least excuse will refuse to convict.

Opening Statement: Use your opening statement to give all the facts of the case to the jury. Some lawyers prefer vague opening statements as a defense against changes in witnesses' testimony. However, *jurors will often forget where they heard a fact, whether from a witness or in opening statement.* First impressions are *often lasting impressions in spite of defense counsel's protestations that the prosecution's opening statement is not evidence.*

Witness: This is one of the areas that has been assigned to the law enforcement agency handling the case. However, some of it will be repeated:

The victim of the crime is usually the first witness called. Taking time to talk with her, explaining the courtroom procedure, and showing her the courtroom will be beneficial to your case. Since it is probable that she will not have seen the defendant since the attack, explain to her she will be asked to identify him in the courtroom. Ask her to point him out in a positive and forceful manner so the jury will not doubt her. Questions which elicit the fear, terror, and humiliation which the victim experienced will help the jury experience these emotions with her and lead to convictions. Tell her to "paint a picture" for the jury so they can understand.

The victim should not remain in the courtroom after testifying. Her presence will be distracting to the jury, and hearing the testimony of other witnesses may be distracting to her. Her presence may also lead the jury to believe the trial is a personal vendetta rather than a criminal case. Care should be taken in argument to stress that *she is a witness to a crime and the State is the plaintiff, not her.*

Presenting other witnesses in chronological order, although not required, makes the case easier for the jury to follow. If you are fortunate enough to have damaging statements which were made by the defendant, use the officer who took them as your final witness. A strong finish is always preferable, especially if no defense is presented.

Expert Witnesses: A new technique in courtroom strategy, if upheld on appeal, could nearly eliminate the problem of juries disbelieving women with no visible signs of resistance. The object is to present rape experts who buttress the victim's testimony that she really did provide adequate resistance even if she wasn't injured. The experts can give an opinion as to what constitutes a reasonable amount of resistance to an assailant, and they could testify that by not resisting past a certain point, a rape victim is precisely following the police department's advice.

In a California case two officers with a sex crimes detail of the police department were qualified as expert witnesses. These expert witnesses testified that the victim's actions—including attempts at passive resistance and running from the house half-naked screaming "I've been raped," afterwards—were entirely consistent with a rape victim's actions. Further, the experts testified that the victim behaved exactly as police department representatives say they should act in such a situation.

The superior court judge in this case stated that the courts should use all the competent help they can get in litigating rape trials. He believes there is a body of knowledge in the issue, amassed by persons who study the crime of rape, that should be used.

Rebuttal: If the defendant takes the stand or presents evidence through other witnesses, one must decide whether or not to present rebuttal testimony: "Generally speaking, bringing back the victim will add little to your case. Most defense attorneys will cover matters they expect the defendant and other witnesses to testify about in their cross-examination of the victim." It should be remembered that the victim should not be recalled unless it is absolutely necessary, since testimony about sexual assaults is extremely stressful for the victim.

Closing Argument: Begin your closing argument with your first witness. It's important to decide the theory of your case early and keep it uppermost in your mind as you present your case, fleshing it out with the responses of your witnesses. The theory and the answers of the witnesses will make up your argument. *Don't anticipate defense arguments in yours.* Something which seems an obvious defense argument may not be so obvious to that person. Deal with his arguments in your rebuttal argument.

When the victim has not been physically injured, juries have a difficult time seeing a sexual assault as a violent crime. *Arguments which stress the criminal acts, the victim's lack of choice, and the continuing fear experienced by the victim, should be used.*

Don't overlook the explanation of the instructions during your argument. Correlating the facts of your case to the instructions help jurors put them in proper perspective. If you have lesser and included offenses, explain them from the *lowest to the highest,* with appropriate facts to support the verdicts. End your explanation with a call for a verdict of the highest offense.

Suggested Consent Instructions: "Before you can find the defendant guilty of the crime of rape, The State must prove, beyond a reasonable doubt, that the sexual intercourse, if any, was accomplished by force or against the will of Jane Doe, and that she did not yield her consent during any part of the act.

"It is not necessary that the force exercised, if any, be only a physical force. Force may consist of such threats and acts as would overcome the will of a woman by fear, provided they are such as to reasonably create apprehension of death or immediate and great bodily harm if she did not submit. Threats and acts need not be expressed verbally and may be implied from conduct.

"On the other hand, if a woman consents during any part of the act of intercourse there is not such opposing will as the law requires to establish the crime of rape. Consent need not be expressed verbally and may be implied from the facts and circumstances shown by the evidence. Where a woman is conscious and in possession of her natural mental and physical powers, is not overpowered by numbers or terrified by threats of immediate and great bodily harm, or when resistance would be useless, she must resist to the extent of her ability.

"In considering whether or not the defendant did have sexual intercourse with the said Jane Doe by force and against her will, you have a right to consider the physical strength and size of the prosecutrix and of the crime, and all other facts and circumstances bearing upon said matter as shown by the evidence."

3. A Note For The Law Enforcement Officer

As a former detective deputy sheriff I can appreciate many of the frustrations of law enforcement officers. This book is written to help you with one major frustration—that of making a good case, only to see it botched by others. The basis of this book is a seminar I give to law enforcement personnel. I have tried to adopt as much of the material as possible in a blueprint to be used by rape victims. Victims of *any* crime feel terribly threatened. Their way of life has been altered—their person or personal effects have been violated to some degree.

After reporting a crime to a law enforcement agency, most victims must wait helplessly for an action by the agency—an action that often never materializes. Often this lack of action on the part of law enforcement officers is unavoidable. But many victims may have the time, sense of urgency, and desire to participate in bringing to justice the criminal who has violated them. Law enforcement officers are prevented from doing many things a "civilian" may do by the Rules of Evidence, and are also restricted from giving certain types of information to "civilians." No such restrictions are placed upon the individual.

Another area I would like to touch is law enforcement officers' attitudes toward the victims of rape.

The Law Enforcement Personality: Law enforcement officers tend to be more conservative politically than the community-at-large and to have a stronger belief in authoritarian values. The great majority hold to a traditional, "double-standard" view of male/female roles, and home and family. In this scheme the home is sacred, men are dominant, women need protection. There are "good women" (wives, mothers, sisters, daughters) and "bad women" (tramps, broads). Bad women drink, swear and entice men. Most people in the criminal justice system believe that "when a woman is bad, she's worse than a man." All of these attitudes will come into play when a law enforcement officer is arresting or aiding a woman.

One lady's burglary may evoke a protective response from the law enforcement officers, and they are both comforting and helpful. They check her house thoroughly to make sure that the burglar is no longer on the premises, examine the forced entrance, ask for a list of missing valuables, and let her know that they are always "on call" if needed.

While women who are arrested are not physically mishandled, they are made to understand that their behavior warrants minimal respect. Most officers go by "If you act like a lady, you'll be treated like a lady." Unfortunately, many female officers adopt the same attitudes.

This "good women"–"bad women" attitude is known as the Madonna–Prostitute Complex. It is an unconscious attitude that is relayed to its recipients through the body language of the officers. Victims reporting a rape often receive the message that they are in the "bad woman" (prostitute) category. Many law enforcement officers are still instructed to thoroughly investigate the character of the victim who reports a rape.

Most law enforcement officers—in fact, most people—still view rape as a sexual act rather than a crime of violence. If a female reports that she has been held up at gun point and forced to give the robber her purse, law enforcement officers would accept the report and investigate it routinely. If this same female reports that she has been held up at gun point and forced to give the robber her purse *and* was raped, a subtle change of attitude can color the officer's investigation. No longer is this female "just another victim." What is her motive? Is she "just a prostitute who didn't get paid?"

Researchers, including myself, have found that not a single rapist cited sexual gratification as the purpose of the rape. So when you think about rape being a sexual instinct, you lose sight of the rapist as a dangerous assailant who feels no guilt about his crimes.

In dealing with victims of rape, if your attitude appears to be that "nothing has happened" to the woman, or if the attitude that "she asked for it" clouds the issue of physical and psychological trauma, then you're sending the message that you feel this way. A special dimension of listening and understanding is to help the victim bear the feelings she's trying to express. To be a "genuine" victim means that one must have people available who can accept and acknowledge that something extremely disruptive has occurred in one's life. In other words, the victim's claim needs confirmation from others.

In dealing with the victim of rape, the officer must be patient and explain what he is doing and why, so that the victim understands the need for each step in the investigative procedure. The officer should offer alternatives, such as, "Would you like to tell me what happened here or would you rather sit down first?" so the victim feels some control in the situation. The victim will be far more willing to cooperate and be able to offer real assistance to the investigation only when it is understood what is needed and why.

A rape victim's family is likely to show emotions ranging from silence to hysteria and vicious anger. The victim's parents, spouse, or lover may react with anger because they feel helpless to correct the situation. That anger may be turned against the victim by blaming the victim for whatever happened. The officer should make sure that someone is present to comfort and be with the victim once his interview has been completed. The officer may contact a relative, close friend, or counselor to be with the victim.

I would like to suggest a source of help that is rarely used by law enforcement agencies: volunteers. They are extensively and successfully used in many organizations. Volunteer fire departments, volunteers in hospitals, Red Cross volunteers, are all examples of successful use of volunteers. Many law enforcement agencies do have viable auxiliary officers, but, the type of volunteer I am suggesting a department use would not fall under their description. There are a lot of people in your town or city who are willing to give time to help officers with rape victims (and other types of victims as well). If you can learn to use these concerned citizens they can save you hours of work—hours that you don't have.

Someone needs to see that the victim is taken care of, and supported throughout the entire legal process. If these counselors are *selected by you,* and *trained by you,* they will be able to obtain information for you that you may not be able to get for many reasons—time being one of these, the emotional condition of the victim being another. You can have these counselors make notes as more information comes out, and you can call these counselors to find out specific answers you find you need, or have forgotten.

These counselors can explain to the victim the various legal processes and delays that can occur from the time an offense is reported to the time the appeals are complete. These counselors can be called when the rape is first reported, and they can remain throughout the long legal process to give emotional support to the victim.

These volunteer counselors may be found in church groups, among retired persons, college students, and service organizations such as women's clubs and N.O.W. Many towns have established rape crisis centers. Unfortunately, many of these crisis centers are at loggerheads with the law enforcement agencies in their communities. All are working toward a common goal, yet working against each other. Although the crisis center and the law enforcement agency may have gotten off on the wrong foot, there is still time to educate these crisis workers to be your helpers, rather than feel they are trying to usurp your authority.

If you select your volunteer counselors you can *spell out exactly what you want*—how they can be of help to you, and *when they are to back off.* If a volunteer is not suitable for your needs, he or she may simply be dropped from the list to be called to counsel victims. Medical personnel, both at the hospitals and in the private offices, can be of great help to law enforcement agencies. Even if the victim does not wish to become involved with the criminal justice system, medical personnel can obtain information from the victim through an assault form that will assist police in establishing an M.O., and give a more accurate record of the actual incidence of rape in your community.

When a law enforcement agency receives a rape report the victim does not wish to prosecute, they will already have someone, the counselor, to turn to for help. And the victim will not feel as though she is being ignored.

Rape is a crime that women are angry about, and we have enough vocal women to do something about this crime. Give these people a chance not only to help the victim, but to educate the public (who make up the jury), and to bring pressure upon prosecutors (who plea bargain for a light sentence) and upon judges (who give lenient sentences) to get the offenders off the street.

Interrogation Records: Many officers and departments keep a log on all of their interrogations, records that can keep an inmate from being granted a new trial: With plenty of time to research, and with a law library inside each prison, inmates send out thousands of writs trying to have their sentences changed. Years after the officer has retired or has forgotten the case, an inmate may send up a writ accusing the officer of denying him his "Rights." The log book should contain the following:

- *Date and time* suspect and investigator *assembled*—their names and the names of any other persons present.
- *Time* suspect was *read his rights* and *signed* the waiver. Witnesses' signatures.
- Time suspect was taken to the rest room, given a smoke, given a drink of water, taken to lunch. Suspect should initial these times.
- *Time interrogation ended.* Repeat for each session.
- A break should be given *at least* every two hours, if possible each hour.

Tips on conducting your interrogation: Each of us will naturally develop our own method of interrogation, but psychiatrists use a method that could be adapted to police use. In order to get the patient to talk, the psychiatrist does not allow the patient to dissipate energy through movement, so the patient's tensions will be relieved through talk. (People who are under pressure often pace the floor, as in a hospital waiting room.)

If your state has an habitual felon statute, be sure to get this criminal's F.B.I. record, and if he qualifies as an habitual offender, document this for the prosecutor.

Appendix 3

The Morals Squad

SEX OFFENDER FILES

The value of appropriate records in the sex crimes phase of operations has been underestimated by many law enforcement agencies.

A critical need for adequate records in this area was brought to the attention of the Rochester, New York, Police Department when a thirteen-year-old girl was murdered. A subsequent review and evaluation of the administrative operations of the police bureau revealed that results were being obtained in sex crimes investigations, but that information of real and substantial value was maintained and kept in five separate areas. These included: (1) detective division files; (2) police women's unit files; (3) records and statistics office files; (4) patrol division files; and (5) the individual personal files of some investigators.

As a result of this review, the morals squad was established. The morals squad consisted of one policewoman, Officer Joan Mathers, and functioned primarily as a fact-finding and research unit on all sex offenses.

A specialized seminar on sex crimes was given by F.B.I. Agent Walter V. McLaughlin to Rochester police. Officers from surrounding departments and agencies were also in attendance. Cooperation and understanding, which might not have been possible, were thereby effected at the beginning of the operations of the morals squad.

William M. Lombard, Chief of Police of Rochester, New York, wrote about this specialized unit in an article, "The Morals Squad," for the July 1965, *FBI Law Enforcement Bulletin.* This excellent article, as valid today as then, is included in this book to help other departments develop their own sex-offender files. Using these procedures, information on any sex offender or offense can be ready reference in one place.

Relative to juvenile sex offenders, these cases most often do not reach the courts. Information concerning juveniles may be received through cooperation with the schools.

MORALS SQUAD DUTIES

The duties of the squad can be described as follows:

Receives and reviews all information daily from all sources within the police bureau on crimes and complaints with a sex motive. This information is gleaned from arrest blotters, daily reports, and direct referrals by investigators.

Reviews all teletype messages regarding sex offenders and offenses.

Maintains complete name, "mug," and related files on all known sex offenders in the metropolitan area.

Solicits information from all other police agencies in the geographic area and renders assistance to them in their investigations whenever requested. (The files are available to all authorized criminal investigators.)

Makes appropriate inquiries of the FBI and the state department of correction to establish recidivism and/or previous sex arrests of local residents which occurred in other jurisdictions.

Cooperates with local probation and state parole offices in receiving information on convicted sex offenders released from custody and residing in the area.

Prepares photos of suspects for investigating officers whenever requested or when a modus operandi of a sex crime is established.

Prepares sex crime pattern reports, which are submitted to commanding officers and units responsible for investigation and apprehension.

Prepares statistical data on sex offenses and offenders in the bureau's jurisdiction.

When the morals squad was set up in Rochester, Policewoman Mathers immediately proceeded to identify sex offenders who had come to the attention of the police bureau during the preceding five years. This first undertaking was a very time-consuming task. Persons arrested on charges of rape, carnal abuse, sodomy, indecent exposure, and endangering the morals of minors were identified through the court dockets for the entire period. Arrest records on cases of assault, disorderly conduct, vagrancy, and intoxication, unearthed another large number of sex-type offenders.

The reports on sex crimes investigations were next thoroughly reviewed, and they served to identify many more offenders who had never been arrested for their immoral acts. Arrests had not been made for any one of several reasons. Among some of the more prevalent reasons for no arrests were: lack of cooperation on the part of the victim or parents of the victim in the investigation and/or in the prosecution of the case; inability to obtain evidence because of prolonged delay or hesitation in reporting the crime; unwillingness on the part of complainant to disclose his or her identity; and the mental state and/or age of the perpetrator.

MASTER FILE

All available information uncovered on these offenders was next incorporated into a master file, alphabetically arranged by last name, to serve as a key index. This file now shows instantly whether a suspect (1) has ever been arrested in the local geographic area or elsewhere for a sex crime, (2) has had any involvement in a sex complaint, or (3) has ever been suspected of being involved.

In a report form, individual items for this file are laid out as follows:

Name
Address
Physical description
Modus operandi
Area of crime
Description of car
License number of car
Special type of crime or perversion
Sex and age of victim
Location of complete investigative report and/or complaint which
    makes this person a suspect

At the top of this report form, there are also noted the police bureau's file number and identifying code number. Noted on the reverse side are arrests, convictions, involvement in investigations, suspicions, probation or parole status, state hospital commitments, teletype messages regarding this offender, and any other pertinent remarks.

The Rochester master file presently contains a total of 2,119 known or suspected sex offenders. There are 1,932 males and 87 females included. Molesters make up the greatest number of offenders with a total of 731 males. Next are male exposers with 372, followed by male homosexuals with 271 names. As of the beginning of 1964, this factfinding morals squad knew that only 82 persons of the total number included in its files were incarcerated in

CODING SYSTEM FOR SEX OFFENDERS
(six digits are being used)

1st Digit	2nd Digit	3rd Digit	4th Digit	5th Digit	6th Digit
COLOR	AGE ACC TO DOB	HEIGHT	BUILD AND HAIR COLOR	HAIR DESCRIPTION	ODDITIES
Code	Code	Code	Code	Code	Code
1· WHITE	1· Before 1900	1· SHORT	1· Slender-Light	1· Straight	1· Limp or Gait
2· NEGRO	2· 1900-1910	2· MEDIUM	2· Slender-Dark	2· Wavy Kinky Curly Wooly	2· Eyes-Glasses
3· OTHER	3· 1910-1920	3· TALL	3· Slender-Grey	3· Bald or Partly Bald	3· Visible Scars Crooked Limbs Deformed Limbs Missing Limbs
	4· 1920-1930		4· Slender-Red		4· Tattoos
	5· 1930-1940		5· Average-Light		5· Speech
	6· 1940-1950		6· Average-Dark		6· Mustache; Beard
	7· 1950-1960		7· Average-Grey		7· Retarded
			8· Average-Red		8· Ears; Hearing
			9· Heavy-Light		9· Teeth
			10· Heavy-Dark		10· Complexion; Moles
			11· Heavy-Grey		11· Left Handed
			12· Heavy-Red		

Figure 1.

local or state institutions. Conversely, there were approximately 2,000 persons with sex-crime potential at large in the area.

PHYSICAL DESCRIPTION FILE

As the Rochester master file grew, it became necessary to establish a code system for rapid identification of logical suspects. It was determined that identification based upon physical description, modus operandi, and area of operation was most practical and desirable. The physical description coding was therefore developed. It has proved to be uncomplicated and workable both as to classification of offender and ease in pinpointing a suspect if the description is developed from a complaint.

The physical description code consists of a six-digit number. Each digit refers to a specific physical characteristic. The digits as they appear in the code number refer to the following physical items:

1st digit—Color (race)
2nd digit—Age (according to date of birth)
3rd digit—Height
4th digit—Build and color of hair
5th digit—Description of hair texture
6th digit—Oddities

The value of each digit differs with variations of a particular physical attribute according to a predetermined codification system. (See fig. 1)

All offenders and suspects in the physical description file are separated into physical likeness groups according to the code. Index card dividers separate groups according to the first two digits in the code number, color and age. The code for each of the subsequent groups follows in order, thus: 1-1-1, 1-1-2, 1-1-3, etc. The last three numbers in the six-digit code narrow down or pinpoint the offender even more exactly. If a victim can tell the police only that the subject was an old man, white, who was tall and talked with an accent, this individual would accordingly be in one of two code groupings, 1-1-3-?-?-5 or 1-2-3-?-?-5.

The investigator of a case is given all pictures in the pertinent groupings to show the victim, and he is advised as to which of these individuals has previously employed a modus operandi similar to that used in the complaint presently under investigation.

In the physical description file, physical oddities are more easily located through a system of colored flags or tabs placed on the index cards. The position and color of the flags on the card highlight the particular oddities or characteristics. (See figs. 2 and 3.)

FLAG POSITIONS IN PHYSICAL DESCRIPTION FILE

ODDITY	1ST POSITION	2ND POSITION	3RD POSITION
1· Limp or Gait			Brown
2· Eyes-Glasses			White
3· Visible Scars, Deformed or Missing Limbs		Red	
4· Tattoos	Blue		
5· Speech	Green		
6· Mustache; Beard	Brown		
7· Retarded			Green
8· Ears; Hearing		Blue	
9· Teeth	White		
10· Complexion: Moles	Red		
11· Left Handed		Brown	

Figure 2.

WHITE

BROWN

Doe, John Joseph
1 "A" Street
C

1-4-2-5-1-1
2
RPD#00000

R

1952 — In Park — whistled at children — dropped trousers below knees
1959 — In High School area — sitting in car — no trousers. Pulled
       across intersection blocking path of teenaged girls

Drives 61 Yellow T Bird   Lic# 3X 412

Born 1926 — 5'9" — 155 Lbs.   — Blond Straight   — Wears Glasses
                                   Hair   Mustache

Figure 3. — Sample card in physical description file. (Third line, upper left, "C" refers to "Convictions"; third line, upper "R" refers to "Recidivism." Brown tab in 1st position; white tab in 3rd position.)

MODUS OPERANDI FILE

A modus operandi file was set up and cross-indexed. All offenders are grouped according to: (1) the act which they have committed, (2) the age- and sex-group violated, (3) local district in which the crime was committed, (4) whether an automobile was used, and (5) whether the offender's occupation enabled him to encounter his victim. One offender may thereby have many cards in this file, covering every facet of the act or acts which he has committed. For example, one offender might have cards under the following groupings in the modus operandi file: exposer, car exposer, park molester, and school area molester.

Modus operandi groupings covered include the following:

Incest
Homosexuality
Sodomy
Boy molesters
Rape
Teenage molesters
Child molesters
Adult molesters
Theater molesters
Park molesters
Bus molesters
School area molesters
    Playgrounds
Downtown area molesters
    Ramp garages
    Midtown plaza
    Department stores
    Parking lots
Girls' dormitory molesters
    University area
    Various nurses' homes
    Girls' boarding houses
Home break-ins with molesting
Exposers
Car exposers
Transvestites
Impersonating
    Police
    Doctor
    Minister

Annoyers
Enticers
Involvement with animals
Cruelty to animals
    Bestiality
Frotteurs
Ladies' underwear involvement
    Stealing
    Wearing
Procurers
Fairy hawks
False alarms
Setting fires
Bombs
Obscene pictures
    Distributing
    Possessing
    Posing
Obscene phone calls
Obscene letters
All written obscenities
Peeping Toms
Prowlers
Sadists
Masochists
Various perversions
    Triolism
    Urolagnia
    Self-abuse
    Foot pervert

Pygmalionism
Bondage

Female offenders are grouped separately. They are classified and filed according to the physical description code system. Prostitutes and Lesbians are special groups in the modus operandi breakdown.

CAR FILE

A car file is also being maintained by the Rochester morals squad. A complete description of each car involved in a sex complaint is classified according to color, license number, and type of complaint against driver. The information is fragmentary, as it is received from criminal investigators and from investigative reports on individual complaints. But by correlating all such information, the morals squad has been able to successfully tie up loose ends and to make available to investigators data on owners of vehicles or suspects in sex crimes. Automobile license numbers which have been reported and found to be illegal are also listed under a separate breakdown. They have proved valuable when subsequent complaints are received and several of the same digits on car plates are reported.

PROWLER FILE

Prowler complaints are filed according to physical descriptions and/or modus operandi, as reported by complaints. These establish patterns of window-peepers, for one thing. The file becomes particularly helpful when a specific area is the scene of a housebreaking-with-sex-motivation. The names of complainants and other pertinent details which might help in effecting an identification are readily available through this file, and the information is given to the investigator working on the housebreaking.

The files of the morals squad remain current because uniformed and plainclothes investigators are under orders to forward all information to the morals squad on persons involved in abnormal sexual behavior, or in suspicious actions of a sexual nature where there is insufficient evidence for an arrest. These facts are incorporated into the files on a continuing basis.

Information on men habitually frequenting and/or loitering about schools, playgrounds, skating rinks, teenage dances, drive-ins, parks, and similar places is solicited and furnished to the morals squad. Youthful males with apparent criminal intent who frequent areas where active homosexuals are known to congregate are of interest to the squad. Information of these types serves to make the files valuable and meaningful, and every bit of such information becomes a part of the files on sex crimes and offenders.

ACCOUNTING PROCEDURE

In addition to the aforementioned files, the morals squad keeps an account of every sex complaint received by the Rochester police bureau. Each complaint is recorded in table form in 10 vertical columns as follows:

1· Location of investigative report (detective division case number).
2· Location of verbatim report of complainant (complaint number).
3· Date of occurrence.
4· Time of day.
5· Complainant and address.
6· Description of subject.
7· Description of car and license number.
8· Location of crime (police district).
9· Modus operandi. (If the subject has been apprehended, his name is also included under the modus operandi column.)
10· Age of victim.

This method of accounting provides a master control and an easy means for compiling totals at the end of each month on both solved and unsolved cases. It has also proved to be most helpful in the determination of sex crime patterns.

CONCLUSIONS

The establishment of a morals squad in the Rochester police bureau was long overdue. We were fortunate to have had an officer available for the assignment who possessed proper interest, enthusiasm, and a great deal of imagination. Most law enforcement agencies have in their ranks an officer who can be utilized in this very important police function.

The absence of physical evidence in most sex crimes dictates the establishment of similar units to correlate and analyze information and complaints. It is a realistic and systematic approach to an ever-present police problem. Public support and confidence in the operation of the units can be gained by making the citizens aware of the true sex crime picture in a community. Periodic news releases, speaking engagements, and public exhibits help to gain such support and confidence.

The morals squad represents a new approach in coping with the problems presented by the sex offenders in our communities. It may be called by a different name in the future, but its duties and functions are here to stay.

Appendix 4

Is Your Handling Fail-Safe?

Ignorance of the law is no excuse when a rapist is acquitted because a technician handled specimens and reports improperly. In the September 1977 issue of *Medical Laboratory Observer,* James A. Terzian, M.D., and Bettina G. Martin, M.S., HT(ASCP), wrote an excellent article on a medico-legal system that will stand up in any court. Their article "Rape Cases: Is Your Test Handling Fail-Safe?" is reprinted here, with permission, to assist those responsible for medical evidence.

"Your hospital laboratory must be able to provide expert clinical evidence and testimony in cases involving an alleged rape. Here's why. Federal crime statistics show that 66,094 rape cases were reported last year in the United States. The charges against many of the defendants in these cases were dismissed prior to trial. Less than 34 percent of the rape cases that did go to trial resulted in convictions. What's going wrong? Many clearly guilty rapists may go free because laboratorians improperly collect or handle evidence that could lead to convictions.

"An effort is now being made in hospitals all across the country to organize health teams that are expertly trained to collect clinical evidence from rape victims. All of us have a key part to play in this effort. We must be especially concerned with the chain of evidence that we collect. This chain is composed of a number of links, with each link representing a systematic procedure performed by a physician or a laboratorian. The first link in this chain is forged when the victim seeks medical attention. The chain becomes complete after all lab reports have been verified, signed, and turned over to the hospital administrator.

"We recently updated our protocol for maintaining the integrity of the

CONTENTS OF THE MEDICO-LEGAL LOCKBOX

FORMS

- Consent for pelvic examination
- Physician's record
- Release of information
- Clinical and anatomical lab requisitions to microbiology immunology, chemistry, and cytology
- Confidential records envelope pre-addressed to the hospital administrator
- (A ballpoint pen is included to complete forms.)

SPECIMEN COLLECTION EQUIPMENT

- Sterile medicine dropper for collection of infant cytology smears and secretions for acid phosphatase
- Plain microslides for cytology and gonococcal smears
- Diamond-tipped pencil for labeling microslides
- Paper clips to separate microslides in fixative
- Cytology fixative (95% alcohol)
- Cardboard slide holder for gonococcal smears
- Culture tubes for microbiology
- Plain blood tubes for chemistry (acid phosphatase)

SPECIMEN RECORD BOOK

The following are to be completed:
- Date and hour of examination
- Patient's name
- Physician's printed name
- Itemized list of all specimens, including the source of each specimen
- Signatures of physician and witness

Figure 1.

chain of evidence in rape cases. Much of the initial work on this protocol was done by Ellie Bechtold, M.D. First we decided that we needed a locked box where reports and specimens taken from the victim could be stored when the clinical pathology attending physician or resident could not immediately examine them. We also needed special containers holding all of the forms and specimen collection equipment that must be readily available when a rape victim is physically examined. Our answer to both needs is the medico-legal lockbox. The contents of the box are show in figure 1.

"Here's how our medico-legal lockbox system works. The attending physician uses the forms inside the box to take the patient's history, obtain signed releases, and order tests. A witness is always present throughout the examination. This witness should be a woman, preferably a nurse or a seasoned laboratorian. We follow these guidelines for obtaining specimens:

"A primary laboratory objective in proving rape is verification that spermatazoa are present in cytological specimens taken from the patient. (Caution: All cytological specimens must be taken by aspiration, to protect spermatazoa from crushing and air-drying.) The presence of acid phosphatase in fluid specimens collected in the examination may be equally acceptable as legal evidence of rape.[1] In most cases we collect medically important smears and cultures for gonococci, and blood for VDRL and alcohol measurements.

"The victim's undergarments and outer clothing may also contain important forensic evidence. Retain those portions of the patient's clothing that you believe contain male ejaculate. Label this evidence. Some police departments prefer to test this evidence in their own laboratories. In other areas, the investigating officer or the prosecutor may ask you to perform these tests. Check with your laboratory director if you are unsure of local requirements. Here's a tip: Do not fold or crumple these suspect garments. Seminal fluid becomes fragile after it dries and must be handled with care to insure verification of the presence of spermatazoa.

"We forge another link in our chain of evidence by labeling each specimen with the victim's full name, the source of each specimen, the determination to be performed, and the date each specimen was taken. The clinical pathology resident distributes these specimens to the appropriate section of the laboratory. The technologist receiving the specimens signs for them in the specimen record book. A written report of these results, verified and signed by an attending pathologist, is then delivered to the medical records depart-

---

1· Schumann, G.B.; Badawy, S.; Peglow, A; and Henry J.B. Prostatic acid phos-acid phosphatase. Current assessment in vaginal fluid of alleged rape victims. *Am. J. Clin. Path.* 66: 944-952, 1976.

ment. Cytology reports are hand-carried to the hospital administrator's office.

"The examining physician forges the final link in our chain of evidence. Each medico-legal box contains an envelope that is pre-addressed to the hospital administrator. The physician places in this envelope the victim's records, the consent form, and the release form. The envelope is sealed and then hand-carried to the hospital administrator's office, where it becomes part of the patient's confidential record.

"Suppose the victim is examined at night, when the hospital is virtually deserted? All important medico-legal specimens and paperwork are locked inside the medico-legal box at the conclusion of the examination. We then place the medico-legal box in a secure area, insuring that the custody will remain unbroken until the hospital administrator and the lab crew arrive. The keys for these boxes, by the way, are kept in the locked narcotics cupboard in the emergency room, in a secured area of the clinical pathology director's office, and in the hospital administrator's office.

"We have several of these medico-legal boxes available so that one of them can be brought back to the laboratory and replenished while others remain available for immediate use. The contents of each box are periodically checked and replenished by technologists or emergency-room personnel.

"At our hospital, the clinical laboratory director and his supervisors are responsible for educating the staff as to the standard operating procedure for the proper handling of evidence in rape cases. A written protocol means nothing unless everyone on the staff fully understands the importance of safeguarding the chain of evidence. We periodically review this written protocol with the day, evening and night staffs. Policy changes are similarly reviewed, with copies of these changes sent for posting in the hospital administration office and in the ER.

"Our inexpensive medico-legal lockbox system is a legally sound approach for preserving a chain of evidence that may be used in court against an accused rapist. Knowing exactly how the system operates, our laboratorians are confident that they won't somehow interfere with the due process of law.